RESTORED to LEAD
Journal

Dr Phillip G Andrade

AUXANO

COPYRIGHTS

RESTORED TO LEAD JOURNAL
Companion to

RESTORED TO LEAD

A Self-Leadership Manual to Break Free from Burnout and Renew Your Purpose

INTRODUCTION

This journal is a companion to the manual called <u>Restored to Lead: A Self-Leadership Manual to Break Free from Burnout and Renew Your Purpose</u>. The items discussed and reflections undertaken in these pages connect directly to the topics introduced in that volume.

This journal is designed to be prayerfully worked on at a regular pace. Five diffrent areas consisting of five pages each are to be worked on per week. The journal has enough pages for a complete year at this pace. However, it is yor journey, so use the sections as you see fit to accomplish the goals the Lord has imressed upon you.

The five unique pages are as follows:

- **Soul Health:** This page covers areas of spiritual growth and a consistent prayer ministry

- **Rhythms and Renewal:** This page continues to assess the dangers of burnout balanced with reflections on a balnaced and healthy lifestyle.

- **Formed for Ministry:** This page helps to integrate ongoing insights from Clinton's leadership emergence theory and ministry margins.

- **Limits and Boundaries:** This page consolidates weekly priorities and practicing healthy boundaries for ministry.

- **Reflections and Joy:** This page is a sort of summary focusing on the discipline of gratitude with a section for general reflection.

It is my prayer that if you use this journal regularly, you will begin to integrate and 'habitualize' the practices that bring joy back into ministry, help you avoid burnout and serve the Lord for the long haul.

Phil

Whatever you do, do your work heartily,

as for the Lord rather than for men,

knowing that from the Lord you will receive the reward of the inheritance.

Colossians 3:23-24

Live for
an Audience
of One

DATE(S) [ ]

SCRIPTURE MEMORY
Focus verse for this week

WORSHIP REFLECTION

How did I practice "often and solitary" time with the Father?

PRAYERS FOR YOUR PEOPLE

The flock entrusted to you.

PRAYERS FOR MY FAMILY

Spouse, children and grandchildren

PRAYERS FOR MYSELF

Personal burdens and requests

Rhythms and Renewal

BURNOUT DANGER LEVEL

Where am I on the road to burnout today?

DAILY RHYTHM CHECK

EXERCISE TODAY?

☐ YES ☐ NO

HEALTHY EATING TODAY?

☐ YES ☐ NO

SPIRITUAL GIFTS PRIMARY?

☐ YES ☐ NO

RESTORATIVE SLEEP?

☐ YES ☐ NO

SABBATH RHYTHM and RENEWAL

What "Protected Space" will I Safeguard this week?

PROCESSING CRITICISM

Discern truth, release falsehood, stay anchored in God's approval.

Formed for Ministry

PROCESS ITEMS CHECK

Rate how God is testing you this week (1-5 scale)

INTEGRITY CHECK
Character Consistency

    (1)   (2)   (3)   (4)   (5)

OBEDIENCE CHECK
Willingness to follow God's lead

    (1)   (2)   (3)   (4)   (5)

WORD CHECK
Applying Scripture to life.

    (1)   (2)   (3)   (4)   (5)

EQUIPPING GOALS

Who am I training or coaching this week? (Moving from doing everything to equipping everyone)

RESPONSIVE MARGIN

How much "white space" have I left in my schedule to weep with those who weep?

Limits and Boundaries

PRIORITIES THIS WEEK (TOP 3)

Focus on predicable rhythmns like sermon prep or startegic thinking.

1

2

3

SECONDARY NEEDS

Tasks that are importnat but not primary.

ITEMS TO DISCUSS WITH A MENTOR

Challenges, Dark Side patterns or relations isolation.

THE ART OF SAYING "NO."

Which digital limits or non-essential requests will I decline to protect my family and soul?

Reflections and Joy

CULTIVATING JOY: 3 ITEMS FOR GRATITUDE

Gratitude guards the heart and restores perspective

1

2

3

GENERAL REFLECTION

Frre-form thoughts, shenanigans, and wound of ministry

INTEGRATION QUESTION

What small adjustment this week moved me toward mental and emotional health?

DATE(S)

SCRIPTURE MEMORY
Focus verse for this week

WORSHIP REFLECTION

How did I practice "often and solitary" time with the Father?

PRAYERS FOR YOUR PEOPLE

The flock entrusted to you.

PRAYERS FOR MY FAMILY

Spouse, children and grandchildren

PRAYERS FOR MYSELF

Personal burdens and requests

Rhythms and Renewal

BURNOUT DANGER LEVEL

Where am I on the road to burnout today?

DAILY RHYTHM CHECK

EXERCISE TODAY?

☐ YES ☐ NO

SPIRITUAL GIFTS PRIMARY?

☐ YES ☐ NO

HEALTHY EATING TODAY?

☐ YES ☐ NO

RESTORATIVE SLEEP?

☐ YES ☐ NO

SABBATH RHYTHM and RENEWAL

What "Protected Space" will I Safeguard this week?

PROCESSING CRITICISM

Discern truth, release falsehood, stay anchored in God's approval.

Formed for Ministry

PROCESS ITEMS CHECK

Rate how God is testing you this week (1-5 scale)

INTEGRITY CHECK
Character Consistency

(1)   (2)   (3)   (4)   (5)

OBEDIENCE CHECK
Willingness to follow God's lead

(1)   (2)   (3)   (4)   (5)

WORD CHECK
Applying Scripture to life.

(1)   (2)   (3)   (4)   (5)

EQUIPPING GOALS

Who am I training or coaching this week? (Moving from doing everything to equipping everyone)

RESPONSIVE MARGIN

How much "white space" have I left in my schedule to weep with those who weep?

Limits and Boundaries

PRIORITIES THIS WEEK (TOP 3)

Focus on predicable rhythmns like sermon prep or startegic thinking.

1

2

3

SECONDARY NEEDS

Tasks that are importnat but not primary.

ITEMS TO DISCUSS WITH A MENTOR

Challenges, Dark Side patterns or relations isolation.

THE ART OF SAYING "NO."

Which digital limits or non-essential requests will I decline to protect my family and soul?

Reflections and Joy

CULTIVATING JOY: 3 ITEMS FOR GRATITUDE

Gratitude guards the heart and restores perspective

1

2

3

GENERAL REFLECTION

Frre-form thoughts, shenanigans, and wound of ministry

INTEGRATION QUESTION

What small adjustment this week moved me toward mental and emotional health?

Soul Health

DATE(S) _____

SCRIPTURE MEMORY
Focus verse for this week

WORSHIP REFLECTION

How did I practice "often and solitary" time with the Father?

PRAYERS FOR YOUR PEOPLE

The flock entrusted to you.

PRAYERS FOR MY FAMILY

Spouse, children and grandchildren

PRAYERS FOR MYSELF

Personal burdens and requests

Rhythms and Renewal

BURNOUT DANGER LEVEL

Where am I on the road to burnout today?

0 1 2 3 4 5 6 7 8 9 10

DAILY RHYTHM CHECK

EXERCISE TODAY?

☐ YES ☐ NO

SPIRITUAL GIFTS PRIMARY?

☐ YES ☐ NO

HEALTHY EATING TODAY?

☐ YES ☐ NO

RESTORATIVE SLEEP?

☐ YES ☐ NO

SABBATH RHYTHM and RENEWAL

What "Protected Space" will I Safeguard this week?

PROCESSING CRITICISM

Discern truth, release falsehood, stay anchored in God's approval.

Formed for Ministry

PROCESS ITEMS CHECK

Rate how God is testing you this week (1-5 scale)

INTEGRITY CHECK
Character Consistency

(1)   (2)   (3)   (4)   (5)

OBEDIENCE CHECK
Willingness to follow God's lead

(1)   (2)   (3)   (4)   (5)

WORD CHECK
Applying Scripture to life.

(1)   (2)   (3)   (4)   (5)

EQUIPPING GOALS

Who am I training or coaching this week? (Moving from doing everything to equipping everyone)

RESPONSIVE MARGIN

How much "white space" have I left in my schedule to weep with those who weep?

Limits and Boundaries

PRIORITIES THIS WEEK (TOP 3)

Focus on predicable rhythmns like sermon prep or startegic thinking.

1

2

3

SECONDARY NEEDS

Tasks that are importnat but not primary.

ITEMS TO DISCUSS WITH A MENTOR

Challenges, Dark Side patterns or relations isolation.

THE ART OF SAYING "NO."

Which digital limits or non-essential requests will I decline to protect my family and soul?

Reflections and Joy

CULTIVATING JOY: 3 ITEMS FOR GRATITUDE

Gratitude guards the heart and restores perspective

1

2

3

GENERAL REFLECTION

Frre-form thoughts, shenanigans, and wound of ministry

INTEGRATION QUESTION

What small adjustment this week moved me toward mental and emotional health?

Soul Health

DATE(S)

SCRIPTURE MEMORY
Focus verse for this week

WORSHIP REFLECTION

How did I practice "often and solitary" time with the Father?

PRAYERS FOR YOUR PEOPLE

The flock entrusted to you.

PRAYERS FOR MY FAMILY

Spouse, children and grandchildren

PRAYERS FOR MYSELF

Personal burdens and requests

Rhythms and Renewal

BURNOUT DANGER LEVEL

Where am I on the road to burnout today?

DAILY RHYTHM CHECK

EXERCISE TODAY?

☐ YES ☐ NO

SPIRITUAL GIFTS PRIMARY?

☐ YES ☐ NO

HEALTHY EATING TODAY?

☐ YES ☐ NO

RESTORATIVE SLEEP?

☐ YES ☐ NO

SABBATH RHYTHM and RENEWAL

What "Protected Space" will I Safeguard this week?

PROCESSING CRITICISM

Discern truth, release falsehood, stay anchored in God's approval.

Formed for Ministry

PROCESS ITEMS CHECK

Rate how God is testing you this week (1-5 scale)

INTEGRITY CHECK
Character Consistency

(1) (2) (3) (4) (5)

OBEDIENCE CHECK
Willingness to follow God's lead

(1) (2) (3) (4) (5)

WORD CHECK
Applying Scripture to life.

(1) (2) (3) (4) (5)

EQUIPPING GOALS

Who am I training or coaching this week? (Moving from doing everything to equipping everyone)

RESPONSIVE MARGIN

How much "white space" have I left in my schedule to weep with those who weep?

Limits and Boundaries

PRIORITIES THIS WEEK (TOP 3)

Focus on predicable rhythmns like sermon prep or startegic thinking.

1

2

3

SECONDARY NEEDS

Tasks that are importnat but not primary.

ITEMS TO DISCUSS WITH A MENTOR

Challenges, Dark Side patterns or relations isolation.

THE ART OF SAYING "NO."

Which digital limits or non-essential requests will I decline to protect my family and soul?

Reflections and Joy

CULTIVATING JOY: 3 ITEMS FOR GRATITUDE

Gratitude guards the heart and restores perspective

1

2

3

GENERAL REFLECTION

Frre-form thoughts, shenanigans, and wound of ministry

INTEGRATION QUESTION

What small adjustment this week moved me toward mental and emotional health?

Soul Health

DATE(S) [   ]

SCRIPTURE MEMORY
Focus verse for this week

WORSHIP REFLECTION

How did I practice "often and solitary" time with the Father?

PRAYERS FOR YOUR PEOPLE

The flock entrusted to you.

PRAYERS FOR MY FAMILY

Spouse, children and grandchildren

PRAYERS FOR MYSELF

Personal burdens and requests

Rhythms and Renewal

BURNOUT DANGER LEVEL

Where am I on the road to burnout today?

DAILY RHYTHM CHECK

EXERCISE TODAY?
☐ YES ☐ NO

SPIRITUAL GIFTS PRIMARY?
☐ YES ☐ NO

HEALTHY EATING TODAY?
☐ YES ☐ NO

RESTORATIVE SLEEP?
☐ YES ☐ NO

SABBATH RHYTHM and RENEWAL

What "Protected Space" will I Safeguard this week?

PROCESSING CRITICISM

Discern truth, release falsehood, stay anchored in God's approval.

Formed for Ministry

PROCESS ITEMS CHECK

Rate how God is testing you this week (1-5 scale)

INTEGRITY CHECK
Character Consistency

(1)　(2)　(3)　(4)　(5)

OBEDIENCE CHECK
Willingness to follow God's lead

(1)　(2)　(3)　(4)　(5)

WORD CHECK
Applying Scripture to life.

(1)　(2)　(3)　(4)　(5)

EQUIPPING GOALS

Who am I training or coaching this week? (Moving from doing everything to equipping everyone)

RESPONSIVE MARGIN

How much "white space" have I left in my schedule to weep with those who weep?

Limits and Boundaries

PRIORITIES THIS WEEK (TOP 3)

Focus on predicable rhythmns like sermon prep or startegic thinking.

1

2

3

SECONDARY NEEDS

Tasks that are importnat but not primary.

ITEMS TO DISCUSS WITH A MENTOR

Challenges, Dark Side patterns or relations isolation.

THE ART OF SAYING "NO."

Which digital limits or non-essential requests will I decline to protect my family and soul?

Reflections and Joy

CULTIVATING JOY: 3 ITEMS FOR GRATITUDE

Gratitude guards the heart and restores perspective

1

2

3

GENERAL REFLECTION

Frre-form thoughts, shenanigans, and wound of ministry

INTEGRATION QUESTION

What small adjustment this week moved me toward mental and emotional health?

Soul Health

DATE(S)

SCRIPTURE MEMORY
Focus verse for this week

WORSHIP REFLECTION

How did I practice "often and solitary" time with the Father?

PRAYERS FOR YOUR PEOPLE

The flock entrusted to you.

PRAYERS FOR MY FAMILY

Spouse, children and grandchildren

PRAYERS FOR MYSELF

Personal burdens and requests

Rhythms and Renewal

BURNOUT DANGER LEVEL

Where am I on the road to burnout today?

DAILY RHYTHM CHECK

EXERCISE TODAY?
☐ YES ☐ NO

SPIRITUAL GIFTS PRIMARY?
☐ YES ☐ NO

HEALTHY EATING TODAY?
☐ YES ☐ NO

RESTORATIVE SLEEP?
☐ YES ☐ NO

SABBATH RHYTHM and RENEWAL

What "Protected Space" will I Safeguard this week?

PROCESSING CRITICISM

Discern truth, release falsehood, stay anchored in God's approval.

Formed for Ministry

PROCESS ITEMS CHECK

Rate how God is testing you this week (1-5 scale)

INTEGRITY CHECK
Character Consistency

(1)   (2)   (3)   (4)   (5)

OBEDIENCE CHECK
Willingness to follow God's lead

(1)   (2)   (3)   (4)   (5)

WORD CHECK
Applying Scripture to life.

(1)   (2)   (3)   (4)   (5)

EQUIPPING GOALS

Who am I training or coaching this week? (Moving from doing everything to equipping everyone)

RESPONSIVE MARGIN

How much "white space" have I left in my schedule to weep with those who weep?

Limits and Boundaries

PRIORITIES THIS WEEK (TOP 3)

Focus on predicable rhythmns like sermon prep or startegic thinking.

1

2

3

SECONDARY NEEDS

Tasks that are importnat but not primary.

ITEMS TO DISCUSS WITH A MENTOR

Challenges, Dark Side patterns or relations isolation.

THE ART OF SAYING "NO."

Which digital limits or non-essential requests will I decline to protect my family and soul?

Reflections and Joy

CULTIVATING JOY: 3 ITEMS FOR GRATITUDE

Gratitude guards the heart and restores perspective

1

2

3

GENERAL REFLECTION

Frre-form thoughts, shenanigans, and wound of ministry

INTEGRATION QUESTION

What small adjustment this week moved me toward mental and emotional health?

DATE(S)

SCRIPTURE MEMORY
Focus verse for this week

WORSHIP REFLECTION

How did I practice "often and solitary" time with the Father?

PRAYERS FOR YOUR PEOPLE

The flock entrusted to you.

PRAYERS FOR MY FAMILY

Spouse, children and grandchildren

PRAYERS FOR MYSELF

Personal burdens and requests

Rhythms and Renewal

BURNOUT DANGER LEVEL

Where am I on the road to burnout today?

DAILY RHYTHM CHECK

EXERCISE TODAY?

☐ YES ☐ NO

HEALTHY EATING TODAY?

☐ YES ☐ NO

SPIRITUAL GIFTS PRIMARY?

☐ YES ☐ NO

RESTORATIVE SLEEP?

☐ YES ☐ NO

SABBATH RHYTHM and RENEWAL

What "Protected Space" will I Safeguard this week?

PROCESSING CRITICISM

Discern truth, release falsehood, stay anchored in God's approval.

Formed for Ministry

PROCESS ITEMS CHECK

Rate how God is testing you this week (1-5 scale)

INTEGRITY CHECK
Character Consistency

(1) (2) (3) (4) (5)

OBEDIENCE CHECK
Willingness to follow God's lead

(1) (2) (3) (4) (5)

WORD CHECK
Applying Scripture to life.

(1) (2) (3) (4) (5)

EQUIPPING GOALS

Who am I training or coaching this week? (Moving from doing everything to equipping everyone)

RESPONSIVE MARGIN

How much "white space" have I left in my schedule to weep with those who weep?

Limits and Boundaries

PRIORITIES THIS WEEK (TOP 3)

Focus on predicable rhythmns like sermon prep or startegic thinking.

1

2

3

SECONDARY NEEDS

Tasks that are importnat but not primary.

ITEMS TO DISCUSS WITH A MENTOR

Challenges, Dark Side patterns or relations isolation.

THE ART OF SAYING "NO."

Which digital limits or non-essential requests will I decline to protect my family and soul?

Reflections and Joy

CULTIVATING JOY: 3 ITEMS FOR GRATITUDE

Gratitude guards the heart and restores perspective

1

2

3

GENERAL REFLECTION

Frre-form thoughts, shenanigans, and wound of ministry

INTEGRATION QUESTION

What small adjustment this week moved me toward mental and emotional health?

DATE(S)

SCRIPTURE MEMORY
Focus verse for this week

WORSHIP REFLECTION

How did I practice "often and solitary" time with the Father?

PRAYERS FOR YOUR PEOPLE

The flock entrusted to you.

PRAYERS FOR MY FAMILY

Spouse, children and grandchildren

PRAYERS FOR MYSELF

Personal burdens and requests

Rhythms and Renewal

BURNOUT DANGER LEVEL

Where am I on the road to burnout today?

DAILY RHYTHM CHECK

EXERCISE TODAY?
☐ YES ☐ NO

SPIRITUAL GIFTS PRIMARY?
☐ YES ☐ NO

HEALTHY EATING TODAY?
☐ YES ☐ NO

RESTORATIVE SLEEP?
☐ YES ☐ NO

SABBATH RHYTHM and RENEWAL

What "Protected Space" will I Safeguard this week?

PROCESSING CRITICISM

Discern truth, release falsehood, stay anchored in God's approval.

Formed for Ministry

PROCESS ITEMS CHECK

Rate how God is testing you this week (1-5 scale)

INTEGRITY CHECK
Character Consistency

(1)　(2)　(3)　(4)　(5)

OBEDIENCE CHECK
Willingness to follow God's lead

(1)　(2)　(3)　(4)　(5)

WORD CHECK
Applying Scripture to life.

(1)　(2)　(3)　(4)　(5)

EQUIPPING GOALS

Who am I training or coaching this week? (Moving from doing everything to equipping everyone)

RESPONSIVE MARGIN

How much "white space" have I left in my schedule to weep with those who weep?

Limits and Boundaries

PRIORITIES THIS WEEK (TOP 3)

Focus on predicable rhythmns like sermon prep or startegic thinking.

1

2

3

SECONDARY NEEDS

Tasks that are importnat but not primary.

ITEMS TO DISCUSS WITH A MENTOR

Challenges, Dark Side patterns or relations isolation.

THE ART OF SAYING "NO."

Which digital limits or non-essential requests will I decline to protect my family and soul?

Reflections and Joy

CULTIVATING JOY: 3 ITEMS FOR GRATITUDE

Gratitude guards the heart and restores perspective

1

2

3

GENERAL REFLECTION

Frre-form thoughts, shenanigans, and wound of ministry

INTEGRATION QUESTION

What small adjustment this week moved me toward mental and emotional health?

DATE(S)

SCRIPTURE MEMORY
Focus verse for this week

WORSHIP REFLECTION

How did I practice "often and solitary" time with the Father?

PRAYERS FOR YOUR PEOPLE

The flock entrusted to you.

PRAYERS FOR MY FAMILY

Spouse, children and grandchildren

PRAYERS FOR MYSELF

Personal burdens and requests

Rhythms and Renewal

BURNOUT DANGER LEVEL

Where am I on the road to burnout today?

DAILY RHYTHM CHECK

EXERCISE TODAY?
[ ] YES [ ] NO

HEALTHY EATING TODAY?
[ ] YES [ ] NO

SPIRITUAL GIFTS PRIMARY?
[ ] YES [ ] NO

RESTORATIVE SLEEP?
[ ] YES [ ] NO

SABBATH RHYTHM and RENEWAL

What "Protected Space" will I Safeguard this week?

PROCESSING CRITICISM

Discern truth, release falsehood, stay anchored in God's approval.

Formed for Ministry

PROCESS ITEMS CHECK

Rate how God is testing you this week (1-5 scale)

INTEGRITY CHECK
Character Consistency

① ② ③ ④ ⑤

OBEDIENCE CHECK
Willingness to follow God's lead

① ② ③ ④ ⑤

WORD CHECK
Applying Scripture to life.

① ② ③ ④ ⑤

EQUIPPING GOALS

Who am I training or coaching this week? (Moving from doing everything to equipping everyone)

RESPONSIVE MARGIN

How much "white space" have I left in my schedule to weep with those who weep?

Limits and Boundaries

PRIORITIES THIS WEEK (TOP 3)

Focus on predicable rhythmns like sermon prep or startegic thinking.

1

2

3

SECONDARY NEEDS

Tasks that are importnat but not primary.

ITEMS TO DISCUSS WITH A MENTOR

Challenges, Dark Side patterns or relations isolation.

THE ART OF SAYING "NO."

Which digital limits or non-essential requests will I decline to protect my family and soul?

Reflections and Joy

CULTIVATING JOY: 3 ITEMS FOR GRATITUDE

Gratitude guards the heart and restores perspective

1

2

3

GENERAL REFLECTION

Frre-form thoughts, shenanigans, and wound of ministry

INTEGRATION QUESTION

What small adjustment this week moved me toward mental and emotional health?

Soul Health

DATE(S)

SCRIPTURE MEMORY
Focus verse for this week

WORSHIP REFLECTION

How did I practice "often and solitary" time with the Father?

PRAYERS FOR YOUR PEOPLE

The flock entrusted to you.

PRAYERS FOR MY FAMILY

Spouse, children and grandchildren

PRAYERS FOR MYSELF

Personal burdens and requests

Rhythms and Renewal

BURNOUT DANGER LEVEL

Where am I on the road to burnout today?

DAILY RHYTHM CHECK

EXERCISE TODAY?
☐ YES ☐ NO

SPIRITUAL GIFTS PRIMARY?
☐ YES ☐ NO

HEALTHY EATING TODAY?
☐ YES ☐ NO

RESTORATIVE SLEEP?
☐ YES ☐ NO

SABBATH RHYTHM and RENEWAL

What "Protected Space" will I Safeguard this week?

PROCESSING CRITICISM

Discern truth, release falsehood, stay anchored in God's approval.

Formed for Ministry

PROCESS ITEMS CHECK

Rate how God is testing you this week (1-5 scale)

INTEGRITY CHECK
Character Consistency

(1) (2) (3) (4) (5)

OBEDIENCE CHECK
Willingness to follow God's lead

(1) (2) (3) (4) (5)

WORD CHECK
Applying Scripture to life.

(1) (2) (3) (4) (5)

EQUIPPING GOALS

Who am I training or coaching this week? (Moving from doing everything to equipping everyone)

RESPONSIVE MARGIN

How much "white space" have I left in my schedule to weep with those who weep?

Limits and Boundaries

PRIORITIES THIS WEEK (TOP 3)

Focus on predicable rhythmns like sermon prep or startegic thinking.

1

2

3

SECONDARY NEEDS

Tasks that are importnat but not primary.

ITEMS TO DISCUSS WITH A MENTOR

Challenges, Dark Side patterns or relations isolation.

THE ART OF SAYING "NO."

Which digital limits or non-essential requests will I decline to protect my family and soul?

Reflections and Joy

CULTIVATING JOY: 3 ITEMS FOR GRATITUDE

Gratitude guards the heart and restores perspective

1

2

3

GENERAL REFLECTION

Frre-form thoughts, shenanigans, and wound of ministry

INTEGRATION QUESTION

What small adjustment this week moved me toward mental and emotional health?

Soul Health

DATE(S)

SCRIPTURE MEMORY
Focus verse for this week

WORSHIP REFLECTION

How did I practice "often and solitary" time with the Father?

PRAYERS FOR YOUR PEOPLE

The flock entrusted to you.

PRAYERS FOR MY FAMILY

Spouse, children and grandchildren

PRAYERS FOR MYSELF

Personal burdens and requests

Rhythms and Renewal

BURNOUT DANGER LEVEL

Where am I on the road to burnout today?

DAILY RHYTHM CHECK

EXERCISE TODAY?

☐ YES ☐ NO

HEALTHY EATING TODAY?

☐ YES ☐ NO

SPIRITUAL GIFTS PRIMARY?

☐ YES ☐ NO

RESTORATIVE SLEEP?

☐ YES ☐ NO

SABBATH RHYTHM and RENEWAL

What "Protected Space" will I Safeguard this week?

PROCESSING CRITICISM

Discern truth, release falsehood, stay anchored in God's approval.

Formed for Ministry

PROCESS ITEMS CHECK

Rate how God is testing you this week (1-5 scale)

INTEGRITY CHECK
Character Consistency

① ② ③ ④ ⑤

OBEDIENCE CHECK
Willingness to follow God's lead

① ② ③ ④ ⑤

WORD CHECK
Applying Scripture to life.

① ② ③ ④ ⑤

EQUIPPING GOALS

Who am I training or coaching this week? (Moving from doing everything to equipping everyone)

RESPONSIVE MARGIN

How much "white space" have I left in my schedule to weep with those who weep?

Limits and Boundaries

PRIORITIES THIS WEEK (TOP 3)

Focus on predicable rhythmns like sermon prep or startegic thinking.

1

2

3

SECONDARY NEEDS

Tasks that are importnat but not primary.

ITEMS TO DISCUSS WITH A MENTOR

Challenges, Dark Side patterns or relations isolation.

THE ART OF SAYING "NO."

Which digital limits or non-essential requests will I decline to protect my family and soul?

Reflections and Joy

CULTIVATING JOY: 3 ITEMS FOR GRATITUDE

Gratitude guards the heart and restores perspective

1

2

3

GENERAL REFLECTION

Frre-form thoughts, shenanigans, and wound of ministry

INTEGRATION QUESTION

What small adjustment this week moved me toward mental and emotional health?

Soul Health

DATE(S)

SCRIPTURE MEMORY
Focus verse for this week

WORSHIP REFLECTION

How did I practice "often and solitary" time with the Father?

PRAYERS FOR YOUR PEOPLE

The flock entrusted to you.

PRAYERS FOR MY FAMILY

Spouse, children and grandchildren

PRAYERS FOR MYSELF

Personal burdens and requests

Rhythms and Renewal

BURNOUT DANGER LEVEL

Where am I on the road to burnout today?

DAILY RHYTHM CHECK

EXERCISE TODAY?
☐ YES ☐ NO

SPIRITUAL GIFTS PRIMARY?
☐ YES ☐ NO

HEALTHY EATING TODAY?
☐ YES ☐ NO

RESTORATIVE SLEEP?
☐ YES ☐ NO

SABBATH RHYTHM and RENEWAL

What "Protected Space" will I Safeguard this week?

PROCESSING CRITICISM

Discern truth, release falsehood, stay anchored in God's approval.

Formed for Ministry

PROCESS ITEMS CHECK

Rate how God is testing you this week (1-5 scale)

INTEGRITY CHECK
Character Consistency

(1) (2) (3) (4) (5)

OBEDIENCE CHECK
Willingness to follow God's lead

(1) (2) (3) (4) (5)

WORD CHECK
Applying Scripture to life.

(1) (2) (3) (4) (5)

EQUIPPING GOALS

Who am I training or coaching this week? (Moving from doing everything to equipping everyone)

RESPONSIVE MARGIN

How much "white space" have I left in my schedule to weep with those who weep?

Limits and Boundaries

PRIORITIES THIS WEEK (TOP 3)

Focus on predicable rhythmns like sermon prep or startegic thinking.

1

2

3

SECONDARY NEEDS

Tasks that are importnat but not primary.

ITEMS TO DISCUSS WITH A MENTOR

Challenges, Dark Side patterns or relations isolation.

THE ART OF SAYING "NO."

Which digital limits or non-essential requests will I decline to protect my family and soul?

Reflections and Joy

CULTIVATING JOY: 3 ITEMS FOR GRATITUDE

Gratitude guards the heart and restores perspective

1

2

3

GENERAL REFLECTION

Frre-form thoughts, shenanigans, and wound of ministry

INTEGRATION QUESTION

What small adjustment this week moved me toward mental and emotional health?

DATE(S) [   ]

SCRIPTURE MEMORY
Focus verse for this week

WORSHIP REFLECTION

How did I practice "often and solitary" time with the Father?

PRAYERS FOR YOUR PEOPLE

The flock entrusted to you.

PRAYERS FOR MY FAMILY

Spouse, children and grandchildren

PRAYERS FOR MYSELF

Personal burdens and requests

Rhythms and Renewal

BURNOUT DANGER LEVEL

Where am I on the road to burnout today?

DAILY RHYTHM CHECK

EXERCISE TODAY?

[ ] YES [ ] NO

SPIRITUAL GIFTS PRIMARY?

[ ] YES [ ] NO

HEALTHY EATING TODAY?

[ ] YES [ ] NO

RESTORATIVE SLEEP?

[ ] YES [ ] NO

SABBATH RHYTHM and RENEWAL

What "Protected Space" will I Safeguard this week?

PROCESSING CRITICISM

Discern truth, release falsehood, stay anchored in God's approval.

Formed for Ministry

PROCESS ITEMS CHECK

Rate how God is testing you this week (1-5 scale)

INTEGRITY CHECK
Character Consistency

①　②　③　④　⑤

OBEDIENCE CHECK
Willingness to follow God's lead

①　②　③　④　⑤

WORD CHECK
Applying Scripture to life.

①　②　③　④　⑤

EQUIPPING GOALS

Who am I training or coaching this week? (Moving from doing everything to equipping everyone)

RESPONSIVE MARGIN

How much "white space" have I left in my schedule to weep with those who weep?

Limits and Boundaries

PRIORITIES THIS WEEK (TOP 3)

Focus on predicable rhythmns like sermon prep or startegic thinking.

1

2

3

SECONDARY NEEDS

Tasks that are importnat but not primary.

ITEMS TO DISCUSS WITH A MENTOR

Challenges, Dark Side patterns or relations isolation.

THE ART OF SAYING "NO."

Which digital limits or non-essential requests will I decline to protect my family and soul?

Reflections and Joy

CULTIVATING JOY: 3 ITEMS FOR GRATITUDE

Gratitude guards the heart and restores perspective

1

2

3

GENERAL REFLECTION

Frre-form thoughts, shenanigans, and wound of ministry

INTEGRATION QUESTION

What small adjustment this week moved me toward mental and emotional health?

Soul Health

DATE(S)

SCRIPTURE MEMORY
Focus verse for this week

WORSHIP REFLECTION

How did I practice "often and solitary" time with the Father?

PRAYERS FOR YOUR PEOPLE

The flock entrusted to you.

PRAYERS FOR MY FAMILY

Spouse, children and grandchildren

PRAYERS FOR MYSELF

Personal burdens and requests

Rhythms and Renewal

BURNOUT DANGER LEVEL

Where am I on the road to burnout today?

DAILY RHYTHM CHECK

EXERCISE TODAY?
☐ YES ☐ NO

SPIRITUAL GIFTS PRIMARY?
☐ YES ☐ NO

HEALTHY EATING TODAY?
☐ YES ☐ NO

RESTORATIVE SLEEP?
☐ YES ☐ NO

SABBATH RHYTHM and RENEWAL

What "Protected Space" will I Safeguard this week?

PROCESSING CRITICISM

Discern truth, release falsehood, stay anchored in God's approval.

Formed for Ministry

PROCESS ITEMS CHECK

Rate how God is testing you this week (1-5 scale)

INTEGRITY CHECK
Character Consistency

(1) (2) (3) (4) (5)

OBEDIENCE CHECK
Willingness to follow God's lead

(1) (2) (3) (4) (5)

WORD CHECK
Applying Scripture to life.

(1) (2) (3) (4) (5)

EQUIPPING GOALS

Who am I training or coaching this week? (Moving from doing everything to equipping everyone)

RESPONSIVE MARGIN

How much "white space" have I left in my schedule to weep with those who weep?

Limits and Boundaries

PRIORITIES THIS WEEK (TOP 3)

Focus on predicable rhythmns like sermon prep or startegic thinking.

1

2

3

SECONDARY NEEDS

Tasks that are importnat but not primary.

ITEMS TO DISCUSS WITH A MENTOR

Challenges, Dark Side patterns or relations isolation.

THE ART OF SAYING "NO."

Which digital limits or non-essential requests will I decline to protect my family and soul?

Reflections and Joy

CULTIVATING JOY: 3 ITEMS FOR GRATITUDE

Gratitude guards the heart and restores perspective

1

2

3

GENERAL REFLECTION

Frre-form thoughts, shenanigans, and wound of ministry

INTEGRATION QUESTION

What small adjustment this week moved me toward mental and emotional health?

Soul Health

DATE(S)

SCRIPTURE MEMORY
Focus verse for this week

WORSHIP REFLECTION

How did I practice "often and solitary" time with the Father?

PRAYERS FOR YOUR PEOPLE

The flock entrusted to you.

PRAYERS FOR MY FAMILY

Spouse, children and grandchildren

PRAYERS FOR MYSELF

Personal burdens and requests

Rhythms and Renewal

BURNOUT DANGER LEVEL

Where am I on the road to burnout today?

DAILY RHYTHM CHECK

EXERCISE TODAY?

[ ] YES   [ ] NO

HEALTHY EATING TODAY?

[ ] YES   [ ] NO

SPIRITUAL GIFTS PRIMARY?

[ ] YES   [ ] NO

RESTORATIVE SLEEP?

[ ] YES   [ ] NO

SABBATH RHYTHM and RENEWAL

What "Protected Space" will I Safeguard this week?

PROCESSING CRITICISM

Discern truth, release falsehood, stay anchored in God's approval.

Formed for Ministry

PROCESS ITEMS CHECK

Rate how God is testing you this week (1-5 scale)

INTEGRITY CHECK
Character Consistency

(1) (2) (3) (4) (5)

OBEDIENCE CHECK
Willingness to follow God's lead

(1) (2) (3) (4) (5)

WORD CHECK
Applying Scripture to life.

(1) (2) (3) (4) (5)

EQUIPPING GOALS

Who am I training or coaching this week? (Moving from doing everything to equipping everyone)

RESPONSIVE MARGIN

How much "white space" have I left in my schedule to weep with those who weep?

Limits and Boundaries

PRIORITIES THIS WEEK (TOP 3)

Focus on predicable rhythmns like sermon prep or startegic thinking.

1

2

3

SECONDARY NEEDS

Tasks that are importnat but not primary.

ITEMS TO DISCUSS WITH A MENTOR

Challenges, Dark Side patterns or relations isolation.

THE ART OF SAYING "NO."

Which digital limits or non-essential requests will I decline to protect my family and soul?

Reflections and Joy

CULTIVATING JOY: 3 ITEMS FOR GRATITUDE

Gratitude guards the heart and restores perspective

1

2

3

GENERAL REFLECTION

Frre-form thoughts, shenanigans, and wound of ministry

INTEGRATION QUESTION

What small adjustment this week moved me toward mental and emotional health?

Soul Health

DATE(S)

SCRIPTURE MEMORY
Focus verse for this week

WORSHIP REFLECTION

How did I practice "often and solitary" time with the Father?

PRAYERS FOR YOUR PEOPLE

The flock entrusted to you.

PRAYERS FOR MY FAMILY

Spouse, children and grandchildren

PRAYERS FOR MYSELF

Personal burdens and requests

Rhythms and Renewal

BURNOUT DANGER LEVEL

Where am I on the road to burnout today?

DAILY RHYTHM CHECK

EXERCISE TODAY?
☐ YES ☐ NO

SPIRITUAL GIFTS PRIMARY?
☐ YES ☐ NO

HEALTHY EATING TODAY?
☐ YES ☐ NO

RESTORATIVE SLEEP?
☐ YES ☐ NO

SABBATH RHYTHM and RENEWAL

What "Protected Space" will I Safeguard this week?

PROCESSING CRITICISM

Discern truth, release falsehood, stay anchored in God's approval.

Formed for Ministry

PROCESS ITEMS CHECK

Rate how God is testing you this week (1-5 scale)

INTEGRITY CHECK
Character Consistency

(1) (2) (3) (4) (5)

OBEDIENCE CHECK
Willingness to follow God's lead

(1) (2) (3) (4) (5)

WORD CHECK
Applying Scripture to life.

(1) (2) (3) (4) (5)

EQUIPPING GOALS

Who am I training or coaching this week? (Moving from doing everything to equipping everyone)

RESPONSIVE MARGIN

How much "white space" have I left in my schedule to weep with those who weep?

Limits and Boundaries

PRIORITIES THIS WEEK (TOP 3)

Focus on predicable rhythmns like sermon prep or startegic thinking.

1

2

3

SECONDARY NEEDS

Tasks that are importnat but not primary.

ITEMS TO DISCUSS WITH A MENTOR

Challenges, Dark Side patterns or relations isolation.

THE ART OF SAYING "NO."

Which digital limits or non-essential requests will I decline to protect my family and soul?

Reflections and Joy

CULTIVATING JOY: 3 ITEMS FOR GRATITUDE

Gratitude guards the heart and restores perspective

1

2

3

GENERAL REFLECTION

Frre-form thoughts, shenanigans, and wound of ministry

INTEGRATION QUESTION

What small adjustment this week moved me toward mental and emotional health?

Soul Health

DATE(S)

SCRIPTURE MEMORY
Focus verse for this week

WORSHIP REFLECTION

How did I practice "often and solitary" time with the Father?

PRAYERS FOR YOUR PEOPLE

The flock entrusted to you.

PRAYERS FOR MY FAMILY

Spouse, children and grandchildren

PRAYERS FOR MYSELF

Personal burdens and requests

Rhythms and Renewal

BURNOUT DANGER LEVEL

Where am I on the road to burnout today?

DAILY RHYTHM CHECK

EXERCISE TODAY?

☐ YES ☐ NO

HEALTHY EATING TODAY?

☐ YES ☐ NO

SPIRITUAL GIFTS PRIMARY?

☐ YES ☐ NO

RESTORATIVE SLEEP?

☐ YES ☐ NO

SABBATH RHYTHM and RENEWAL

What "Protected Space" will I Safeguard this week?

PROCESSING CRITICISM

Discern truth, release falsehood, stay anchored in God's approval.

Formed for Ministry

PROCESS ITEMS CHECK

Rate how God is testing you this week (1-5 scale)

INTEGRITY CHECK
Character Consistency

(1)　(2)　(3)　(4)　(5)

OBEDIENCE CHECK
Willingness to follow God's lead

(1)　(2)　(3)　(4)　(5)

WORD CHECK
Applying Scripture to life.

(1)　(2)　(3)　(4)　(5)

EQUIPPING GOALS

Who am I training or coaching this week? (Moving from doing everything to equipping everyone)

RESPONSIVE MARGIN

How much "white space" have I left in my schedule to weep with those who weep?

Limits and Boundaries

PRIORITIES THIS WEEK (TOP 3)

Focus on predicable rhythmns like sermon prep or startegic thinking.

1

2

3

SECONDARY NEEDS

Tasks that are importnat but not primary.

ITEMS TO DISCUSS WITH A MENTOR

Challenges, Dark Side patterns or relations isolation.

THE ART OF SAYING "NO."

Which digital limits or non-essential requests will I decline to protect my family and soul?

Reflections and Joy

CULTIVATING JOY: 3 ITEMS FOR GRATITUDE

Gratitude guards the heart and restores perspective

1

2

3

GENERAL REFLECTION

Frre-form thoughts, shenanigans, and wound of ministry

INTEGRATION QUESTION

What small adjustment this week moved me toward mental and emotional health?

DATE(S)

SCRIPTURE MEMORY
Focus verse for this week

WORSHIP REFLECTION

How did I practice "often and solitary" time with the Father?

PRAYERS FOR YOUR PEOPLE

The flock entrusted to you.

PRAYERS FOR MY FAMILY

Spouse, children and grandchildren

PRAYERS FOR MYSELF

Personal burdens and requests

Rhythms and Renewal

BURNOUT DANGER LEVEL

Where am I on the road to burnout today?

DAILY RHYTHM CHECK

EXERCISE TODAY?

☐ YES ☐ NO

SPIRITUAL GIFTS PRIMARY?

☐ YES ☐ NO

HEALTHY EATING TODAY?

☐ YES ☐ NO

RESTORATIVE SLEEP?

☐ YES ☐ NO

SABBATH RHYTHM and RENEWAL

What "Protected Space" will I Safeguard this week?

PROCESSING CRITICISM

Discern truth, release falsehood, stay anchored in God's approval.

Formed for Ministry

PROCESS ITEMS CHECK

Rate how God is testing you this week (1-5 scale)

INTEGRITY CHECK
Character Consistency

(1) (2) (3) (4) (5)

OBEDIENCE CHECK
Willingness to follow God's lead

(1) (2) (3) (4) (5)

WORD CHECK
Applying Scripture to life.

(1) (2) (3) (4) (5)

EQUIPPING GOALS

Who am I training or coaching this week? (Moving from doing everything to equipping everyone)

RESPONSIVE MARGIN

How much "white space" have I left in my schedule to weep with those who weep?

Limits and Boundaries

PRIORITIES THIS WEEK (TOP 3)

Focus on predicable rhythmns like sermon prep or startegic thinking.

1

2

3

SECONDARY NEEDS

Tasks that are importnat but not primary.

ITEMS TO DISCUSS WITH A MENTOR

Challenges, Dark Side patterns or relations isolation.

THE ART OF SAYING "NO."

Which digital limits or non-essential requests will I decline to protect my family and soul?

Reflections and Joy

CULTIVATING JOY: 3 ITEMS FOR GRATITUDE

Gratitude guards the heart and restores perspective

1

2

3

GENERAL REFLECTION

Frre-form thoughts, shenanigans, and wound of ministry

INTEGRATION QUESTION

What small adjustment this week moved me toward mental and emotional health?

Soul Health

DATE(S)

SCRIPTURE MEMORY
Focus verse for this week

WORSHIP REFLECTION

How did I practice "often and solitary" time with the Father?

PRAYERS FOR YOUR PEOPLE

The flock entrusted to you.

PRAYERS FOR MY FAMILY

Spouse, children and grandchildren

PRAYERS FOR MYSELF

Personal burdens and requests

Rhythms and Renewal

BURNOUT DANGER LEVEL

Where am I on the road to burnout today?

DAILY RHYTHM CHECK

EXERCISE TODAY?

☐ YES ☐ NO

SPIRITUAL GIFTS PRIMARY?

☐ YES ☐ NO

HEALTHY EATING TODAY?

☐ YES ☐ NO

RESTORATIVE SLEEP?

☐ YES ☐ NO

SABBATH RHYTHM and RENEWAL

What "Protected Space" will I Safeguard this week?

PROCESSING CRITICISM

Discern truth, release falsehood, stay anchored in God's approval.

Formed for Ministry

PROCESS ITEMS CHECK

Rate how God is testing you this week (1-5 scale)

INTEGRITY CHECK
Character Consistency
(1) (2) (3) (4) (5)

OBEDIENCE CHECK
Willingness to follow God's lead
(1) (2) (3) (4) (5)

WORD CHECK
Applying Scripture to life.
(1) (2) (3) (4) (5)

EQUIPPING GOALS

Who am I training or coaching this week? (Moving from doing everything to equipping everyone)

RESPONSIVE MARGIN

How much "white space" have I left in my schedule to weep with those who weep?

Limits and Boundaries

PRIORITIES THIS WEEK (TOP 3)

Focus on predicable rhythmns like sermon prep or startegic thinking.

1

2

3

SECONDARY NEEDS

Tasks that are importnat but not primary.

ITEMS TO DISCUSS WITH A MENTOR

Challenges, Dark Side patterns or relations isolation.

THE ART OF SAYING "NO."

Which digital limits or non-essential requests will I decline to protect my family and soul?

Reflections and Joy

CULTIVATING JOY: 3 ITEMS FOR GRATITUDE

Gratitude guards the heart and restores perspective

1

2

3

GENERAL REFLECTION

Frre-form thoughts, shenanigans, and wound of ministry

INTEGRATION QUESTION

What small adjustment this week moved me toward mental and emotional health?

Soul Health

DATE(S)

SCRIPTURE MEMORY
Focus verse for this week

WORSHIP REFLECTION

How did I practice "often and solitary" time with the Father?

PRAYERS FOR YOUR PEOPLE

The flock entrusted to you.

PRAYERS FOR MY FAMILY

Spouse, children and grandchildren

PRAYERS FOR MYSELF

Personal burdens and requests

Rhythms and Renewal

BURNOUT DANGER LEVEL

Where am I on the road to burnout today?

DAILY RHYTHM CHECK

EXERCISE TODAY?
☐ YES ☐ NO

SPIRITUAL GIFTS PRIMARY?
☐ YES ☐ NO

HEALTHY EATING TODAY?
☐ YES ☐ NO

RESTORATIVE SLEEP?
☐ YES ☐ NO

SABBATH RHYTHM and RENEWAL

What "Protected Space" will I Safeguard this week?

PROCESSING CRITICISM

Discern truth, release falsehood, stay anchored in God's approval.

Formed for Ministry

PROCESS ITEMS CHECK

Rate how God is testing you this week (1-5 scale)

INTEGRITY CHECK
Character Consistency

(1) (2) (3) (4) (5)

OBEDIENCE CHECK
Willingness to follow God's lead

(1) (2) (3) (4) (5)

WORD CHECK
Applying Scripture to life.

(1) (2) (3) (4) (5)

EQUIPPING GOALS

Who am I training or coaching this week? (Moving from doing everything to equipping everyone)

RESPONSIVE MARGIN

How much "white space" have I left in my schedule to weep with those who weep?

Limits and Boundaries

PRIORITIES THIS WEEK (TOP 3)

Focus on predicable rhythmns like sermon prep or startegic thinking.

1

2

3

SECONDARY NEEDS

Tasks that are importnat but not primary.

ITEMS TO DISCUSS WITH A MENTOR

Challenges, Dark Side patterns or relations isolation.

THE ART OF SAYING "NO."

Which digital limits or non-essential requests will I decline to protect my family and soul?

Reflections and Joy

CULTIVATING JOY: 3 ITEMS FOR GRATITUDE

Gratitude guards the heart and restores perspective

1

2

3

GENERAL REFLECTION

Frre-form thoughts, shenanigans, and wound of ministry

INTEGRATION QUESTION

What small adjustment this week moved me toward mental and emotional health?

DATE(S) [ ]

SCRIPTURE MEMORY
Focus verse for this week

WORSHIP REFLECTION

How did I practice "often and solitary" time with the Father?

PRAYERS FOR YOUR PEOPLE

The flock entrusted to you.

PRAYERS FOR MY FAMILY

Spouse, children and grandchildren

PRAYERS FOR MYSELF

Personal burdens and requests

Rhythms and Renewal

BURNOUT DANGER LEVEL

Where am I on the road to burnout today?

DAILY RHYTHM CHECK

EXERCISE TODAY?
☐ YES ☐ NO

SPIRITUAL GIFTS PRIMARY?
☐ YES ☐ NO

HEALTHY EATING TODAY?
☐ YES ☐ NO

RESTORATIVE SLEEP?
☐ YES ☐ NO

SABBATH RHYTHM and RENEWAL

What "Protected Space" will I Safeguard this week?

PROCESSING CRITICISM

Discern truth, release falsehood, stay anchored in God's approval.

Formed for Ministry

PROCESS ITEMS CHECK

Rate how God is testing you this week (1-5 scale)

INTEGRITY CHECK
Character Consistency

(1)   (2)   (3)   (4)   (5)

OBEDIENCE CHECK
Willingness to follow God's lead

(1)   (2)   (3)   (4)   (5)

WORD CHECK
Applying Scripture to life.

(1)   (2)   (3)   (4)   (5)

EQUIPPING GOALS

Who am I training or coaching this week? (Moving from doing everything to equipping everyone)

RESPONSIVE MARGIN

How much "white space" have I left in my schedule to weep with those who weep?

Limits and Boundaries

PRIORITIES THIS WEEK (TOP 3)

Focus on predicable rhythmns like sermon prep or startegic thinking.

1

2

3

SECONDARY NEEDS

Tasks that are importnat but not primary.

ITEMS TO DISCUSS WITH A MENTOR

Challenges, Dark Side patterns or relations isolation.

THE ART OF SAYING "NO."

Which digital limits or non-essential requests will I decline to protect my family and soul?

Reflections and Joy

CULTIVATING JOY: 3 ITEMS FOR GRATITUDE

Gratitude guards the heart and restores perspective

1

2

3

GENERAL REFLECTION

Frre-form thoughts, shenanigans, and wound of ministry

INTEGRATION QUESTION

What small adjustment this week moved me toward mental and emotional health?

Soul Health

DATE(S)

SCRIPTURE MEMORY
Focus verse for this week

WORSHIP REFLECTION

How did I practice "often and solitary" time with the Father?

PRAYERS FOR YOUR PEOPLE

The flock entrusted to you.

PRAYERS FOR MY FAMILY

Spouse, children and grandchildren

PRAYERS FOR MYSELF

Personal burdens and requests

Rhythms and Renewal

BURNOUT DANGER LEVEL

Where am I on the road to burnout today?

DAILY RHYTHM CHECK

EXERCISE TODAY?

☐ YES ☐ NO

SPIRITUAL GIFTS PRIMARY?

☐ YES ☐ NO

HEALTHY EATING TODAY?

☐ YES ☐ NO

RESTORATIVE SLEEP?

☐ YES ☐ NO

SABBATH RHYTHM and RENEWAL

What "Protected Space" will I Safeguard this week?

PROCESSING CRITICISM

Discern truth, release falsehood, stay anchored in God's approval.

Formed for Ministry

PROCESS ITEMS CHECK

Rate how God is testing you this week (1-5 scale)

INTEGRITY CHECK
Character Consistency

(1) (2) (3) (4) (5)

OBEDIENCE CHECK
Willingness to follow God's lead

(1) (2) (3) (4) (5)

WORD CHECK
Applying Scripture to life.

(1) (2) (3) (4) (5)

EQUIPPING GOALS

Who am I training or coaching this week? (Moving from doing everything to equipping everyone)

RESPONSIVE MARGIN

How much "white space" have I left in my schedule to weep with those who weep?

Limits and Boundaries

PRIORITIES THIS WEEK (TOP 3)

Focus on predicable rhythmns like sermon prep or startegic thinking.

1

2

3

SECONDARY NEEDS

Tasks that are importnat but not primary.

ITEMS TO DISCUSS WITH A MENTOR

Challenges, Dark Side patterns or relations isolation.

THE ART OF SAYING "NO."

Which digital limits or non-essential requests will I decline to protect my family and soul?

Reflections and Joy

CULTIVATING JOY: 3 ITEMS FOR GRATITUDE

Gratitude guards the heart and restores perspective

1

2

3

GENERAL REFLECTION

Frre-form thoughts, shenanigans, and wound of ministry

INTEGRATION QUESTION

What small adjustment this week moved me toward mental and emotional health?

Soul Health

DATE(S) [ ]

SCRIPTURE MEMORY
Focus verse for this week

WORSHIP REFLECTION

How did I practice "often and solitary" time with the Father?

PRAYERS FOR YOUR PEOPLE

The flock entrusted to you.

PRAYERS FOR MY FAMILY

Spouse, children and grandchildren

PRAYERS FOR MYSELF

Personal burdens and requests

Rhythms and Renewal

BURNOUT DANGER LEVEL

Where am I on the road to burnout today?

DAILY RHYTHM CHECK

EXERCISE TODAY?

[ ] YES   [ ] NO

HEALTHY EATING TODAY?

[ ] YES   [ ] NO

SPIRITUAL GIFTS PRIMARY?

[ ] YES   [ ] NO

RESTORATIVE SLEEP?

[ ] YES   [ ] NO

SABBATH RHYTHM and RENEWAL

What "Protected Space" will I Safeguard this week?

PROCESSING CRITICISM

Discern truth, release falsehood, stay anchored in God's approval.

Formed for Ministry

PROCESS ITEMS CHECK

Rate how God is testing you this week (1-5 scale)

INTEGRITY CHECK
Character Consistency

(1) (2) (3) (4) (5)

OBEDIENCE CHECK
Willingness to follow God's lead

(1) (2) (3) (4) (5)

WORD CHECK
Applying Scripture to life.

(1) (2) (3) (4) (5)

EQUIPPING GOALS

Who am I training or coaching this week? (Moving from doing everything to equipping everyone)

RESPONSIVE MARGIN

How much "white space" have I left in my schedule to weep with those who weep?

Limits and Boundaries

PRIORITIES THIS WEEK (TOP 3)

Focus on predicable rhythmns like sermon prep or startegic thinking.

1

2

3

SECONDARY NEEDS

Tasks that are importnat but not primary.

ITEMS TO DISCUSS WITH A MENTOR

Challenges, Dark Side patterns or relations isolation.

THE ART OF SAYING "NO."

Which digital limits or non-essential requests will I decline to protect my family and soul?

Reflections and Joy

CULTIVATING JOY: 3 ITEMS FOR GRATITUDE

Gratitude guards the heart and restores perspective

1

2

3

GENERAL REFLECTION

Frre form thoughts, shenanigans, and wound of ministry

INTEGRATION QUESTION

What small adjustment this week moved me toward mental and emotional health?

DATE(S) [   ]

SCRIPTURE MEMORY
Focus verse for this week

WORSHIP REFLECTION

How did I practice "often and solitary" time with the Father?

PRAYERS FOR YOUR PEOPLE

The flock entrusted to you.

PRAYERS FOR MY FAMILY

Spouse, children and grandchildren

PRAYERS FOR MYSELF

Personal burdens and requests

Rhythms and Renewal

BURNOUT DANGER LEVEL

Where am I on the road to burnout today?

DAILY RHYTHM CHECK

EXERCISE TODAY?
☐ YES ☐ NO

SPIRITUAL GIFTS PRIMARY?
☐ YES ☐ NO

HEALTHY EATING TODAY?
☐ YES ☐ NO

RESTORATIVE SLEEP?
☐ YES ☐ NO

SABBATH RHYTHM and RENEWAL

What "Protected Space" will I Safeguard this week?

PROCESSING CRITICISM

Discern truth, release falsehood, stay anchored in God's approval.

Formed for Ministry

PROCESS ITEMS CHECK

Rate how God is testing you this week (1-5 scale)

INTEGRITY CHECK
Character Consistency

(1) (2) (3) (4) (5)

OBEDIENCE CHECK
Willingness to follow God's lead

(1) (2) (3) (4) (5)

WORD CHECK
Applying Scripture to life.

(1) (2) (3) (4) (5)

EQUIPPING GOALS

Who am I training or coaching this week? (Moving from doing everything to equipping everyone)

RESPONSIVE MARGIN

How much "white space" have I left in my schedule to weep with those who weep?

Limits and Boundaries

PRIORITIES THIS WEEK (TOP 3)

Focus on predicable rhythmns like sermon prep or startegic thinking.

1

2

3

SECONDARY NEEDS

Tasks that are importnat but not primary.

ITEMS TO DISCUSS WITH A MENTOR

Challenges, Dark Side patterns or relations isolation.

THE ART OF SAYING "NO."

Which digital limits or non-essential requests will I decline to protect my family and soul?

Reflections and Joy

CULTIVATING JOY: 3 ITEMS FOR GRATITUDE

Gratitude guards the heart and restores perspective

1

2

3

GENERAL REFLECTION

Frre-form thoughts, shenanigans, and wound of ministry

INTEGRATION QUESTION

What small adjustment this week moved me toward mental and emotional health?

Soul Health

DATE(S)

SCRIPTURE MEMORY
Focus verse for this week

WORSHIP REFLECTION

How did I practice "often and solitary" time with the Father?

PRAYERS FOR YOUR PEOPLE

The flock entrusted to you.

PRAYERS FOR MY FAMILY

Spouse, children and grandchildren

PRAYERS FOR MYSELF

Personal burdens and requests

Rhythms and Renewal

BURNOUT DANGER LEVEL

Where am I on the road to burnout today?

DAILY RHYTHM CHECK

EXERCISE TODAY?
☐ YES ☐ NO

SPIRITUAL GIFTS PRIMARY?
☐ YES ☐ NO

HEALTHY EATING TODAY?
☐ YES ☐ NO

RESTORATIVE SLEEP?
☐ YES ☐ NO

SABBATH RHYTHM and RENEWAL

What "Protected Space" will I Safeguard this week?

PROCESSING CRITICISM

Discern truth, release falsehood, stay anchored in God's approval.

Formed for Ministry

PROCESS ITEMS CHECK

Rate how God is testing you this week (1-5 scale)

INTEGRITY CHECK
Character Consistency

(1)   (2)   (3)   (4)   (5)

OBEDIENCE CHECK
Willingness to follow God's lead

(1)   (2)   (3)   (4)   (5)

WORD CHECK
Applying Scripture to life.

(1)   (2)   (3)   (4)   (5)

EQUIPPING GOALS

Who am I training or coaching this week? (Moving from doing everything to equipping everyone)

RESPONSIVE MARGIN

How much "white space" have I left in my schedule to weep with those who weep?

Limits and Boundaries

PRIORITIES THIS WEEK (TOP 3)

Focus on predicable rhythmns like sermon prep or startegic thinking.

1

2

3

SECONDARY NEEDS

Tasks that are importnat but not primary.

ITEMS TO DISCUSS WITH A MENTOR

Challenges, Dark Side patterns or relations isolation.

THE ART OF SAYING "NO."

Which digital limits or non-essential requests will I decline to protect my family and soul?

Reflections and Joy

CULTIVATING JOY: 3 ITEMS FOR GRATITUDE

Gratitude guards the heart and restores perspective

1

2

3

GENERAL REFLECTION

Frre-form thoughts, shenanigans, and wound of ministry

INTEGRATION QUESTION

What small adjustment this week moved me toward mental and emotional health?

Soul Health

DATE(S)

SCRIPTURE MEMORY
Focus verse for this week

WORSHIP REFLECTION

How did I practice "often and solitary" time with the Father?

PRAYERS FOR YOUR PEOPLE

The flock entrusted to you.

PRAYERS FOR MY FAMILY

Spouse, children and grandchildren

PRAYERS FOR MYSELF

Personal burdens and requests

Rhythms and Renewal

BURNOUT DANGER LEVEL

Where am I on the road to burnout today?

DAILY RHYTHM CHECK

EXERCISE TODAY?

☐ YES ☐ NO

SPIRITUAL GIFTS PRIMARY?

☐ YES ☐ NO

HEALTHY EATING TODAY?

☐ YES ☐ NO

RESTORATIVE SLEEP?

☐ YES ☐ NO

SABBATH RHYTHM and RENEWAL

What "Protected Space" will I Safeguard this week?

PROCESSING CRITICISM

Discern truth, release falsehood, stay anchored in God's approval.

Formed for Ministry

PROCESS ITEMS CHECK

Rate how God is testing you this week (1-5 scale)

INTEGRITY CHECK
Character Consistency

(1) (2) (3) (4) (5)

OBEDIENCE CHECK
Willingness to follow God's lead

(1) (2) (3) (4) (5)

WORD CHECK
Applying Scripture to life.

(1) (2) (3) (4) (5)

EQUIPPING GOALS

Who am I training or coaching this week? (Moving from doing everything to equipping everyone)

RESPONSIVE MARGIN

How much "white space" have I left in my schedule to weep with those who weep?

Limits and Boundaries

PRIORITIES THIS WEEK (TOP 3)

Focus on predicable rhythmns like sermon prep or startegic thinking.

1

2

3

SECONDARY NEEDS

Tasks that are importnat but not primary.

ITEMS TO DISCUSS WITH A MENTOR

Challenges, Dark Side patterns or relations isolation.

THE ART OF SAYING "NO."

Which digital limits or non-essential requests will I decline to protect my family and soul?

Reflections and Joy

CULTIVATING JOY: 3 ITEMS FOR GRATITUDE

Gratitude guards the heart and restores perspective

1

2

3

GENERAL REFLECTION

Frre-form thoughts, shenanigans, and wound of ministry

INTEGRATION QUESTION

What small adjustment this week moved me toward mental and emotional health?

Soul Health

DATE(S)

SCRIPTURE MEMORY
Focus verse for this week

WORSHIP REFLECTION

How did I practice "often and solitary" time with the Father?

PRAYERS FOR YOUR PEOPLE

The flock entrusted to you.

PRAYERS FOR MY FAMILY

Spouse, children and grandchildren

PRAYERS FOR MYSELF

Personal burdens and requests

Rhythms and Renewal

BURNOUT DANGER LEVEL

Where am I on the road to burnout today?

DAILY RHYTHM CHECK

EXERCISE TODAY?

☐ YES ☐ NO

SPIRITUAL GIFTS PRIMARY?

☐ YES ☐ NO

HEALTHY EATING TODAY?

☐ YES ☐ NO

RESTORATIVE SLEEP?

☐ YES ☐ NO

SABBATH RHYTHM and RENEWAL

What "Protected Space" will I Safeguard this week?

PROCESSING CRITICISM

Discern truth, release falsehood, stay anchored in God's approval.

Formed for Ministry

PROCESS ITEMS CHECK

Rate how God is testing you this week (1-5 scale)

INTEGRITY CHECK
Character Consistency

(1) (2) (3) (4) (5)

OBEDIENCE CHECK
Willingness to follow God's lead

(1) (2) (3) (4) (5)

WORD CHECK
Applying Scripture to life.

(1) (2) (3) (4) (5)

EQUIPPING GOALS

Who am I training or coaching this week? (Moving from doing everything to equipping everyone)

RESPONSIVE MARGIN

How much "white space" have I left in my schedule to weep with those who weep?

Limits and Boundaries

PRIORITIES THIS WEEK (TOP 3)

Focus on predicable rhythmns like sermon prep or startegic thinking.

1

2

3

SECONDARY NEEDS

Tasks that are importnat but not primary.

ITEMS TO DISCUSS WITH A MENTOR

Challenges, Dark Side patterns or relations isolation.

THE ART OF SAYING "NO."

Which digital limits or non-essential requests will I decline to protect my family and soul?

Reflections and Joy

CULTIVATING JOY: 3 ITEMS FOR GRATITUDE

Gratitude guards the heart and restores perspective

1

2

3

GENERAL REFLECTION

Frre-form thoughts, shenanigans, and wound of ministry

INTEGRATION QUESTION

What small adjustment this week moved me toward mental and emotional health?

DATE(S)

SCRIPTURE MEMORY
Focus verse for this week

WORSHIP REFLECTION

How did I practice "often and solitary" time with the Father?

PRAYERS FOR YOUR PEOPLE

The flock entrusted to you.

PRAYERS FOR MY FAMILY

Spouse, children and grandchildren

PRAYERS FOR MYSELF

Personal burdens and requests

Rhythms and Renewal

BURNOUT DANGER LEVEL

Where am I on the road to burnout today?

DAILY RHYTHM CHECK

EXERCISE TODAY?
☐ YES ☐ NO

SPIRITUAL GIFTS PRIMARY?
☐ YES ☐ NO

HEALTHY EATING TODAY?
☐ YES ☐ NO

RESTORATIVE SLEEP?
☐ YES ☐ NO

SABBATH RHYTHM and RENEWAL

What "Protected Space" will I Safeguard this week?

PROCESSING CRITICISM

Discern truth, release falsehood, stay anchored in God's approval.

Formed for Ministry

PROCESS ITEMS CHECK

Rate how God is testing you this week (1-5 scale)

INTEGRITY CHECK
Character Consistency

(1) (2) (3) (4) (5)

OBEDIENCE CHECK
Willingness to follow God's lead

(1) (2) (3) (4) (5)

WORD CHECK
Applying Scripture to life.

(1) (2) (3) (4) (5)

EQUIPPING GOALS

Who am I training or coaching this week? (Moving from doing everything to equipping everyone)

RESPONSIVE MARGIN

How much "white space" have I left in my schedule to weep with those who weep?

Limits and Boundaries

PRIORITIES THIS WEEK (TOP 3)

Focus on predicable rhythmns like sermon prep or startegic thinking.

1

2

3

SECONDARY NEEDS

Tasks that are importnat but not primary.

ITEMS TO DISCUSS WITH A MENTOR

Challenges, Dark Side patterns or relations isolation.

THE ART OF SAYING "NO."

Which digital limits or non-essential requests will I decline to protect my family and soul?

Reflections and Joy

CULTIVATING JOY: 3 ITEMS FOR GRATITUDE

Gratitude guards the heart and restores perspective

1

2

3

GENERAL REFLECTION

Frre-form thoughts, shenanigans, and wound of ministry

INTEGRATION QUESTION

What small adjustment this week moved me toward mental and emotional health?

Soul Health

DATE(S) [   ]

SCRIPTURE MEMORY
Focus verse for this week

WORSHIP REFLECTION

How did I practice "often and solitary" time with the Father?

PRAYERS FOR YOUR PEOPLE

The flock entrusted to you.

PRAYERS FOR MY FAMILY

Spouse, children and grandchildren

PRAYERS FOR MYSELF

Personal burdens and requests

Rhythms and Renewal

BURNOUT DANGER LEVEL

Where am I on the road to burnout today?

DAILY RHYTHM CHECK

EXERCISE TODAY?

☐ YES ☐ NO

SPIRITUAL GIFTS PRIMARY?

☐ YES ☐ NO

HEALTHY EATING TODAY?

☐ YES ☐ NO

RESTORATIVE SLEEP?

☐ YES ☐ NO

SABBATH RHYTHM and RENEWAL

What "Protected Space" will I Safeguard this week?

PROCESSING CRITICISM

Discern truth, release falsehood, stay anchored in God's approval.

Formed for Ministry

PROCESS ITEMS CHECK

Rate how God is testing you this week (1-5 scale)

INTEGRITY CHECK
Character Consistency

(1) (2) (3) (4) (5)

OBEDIENCE CHECK
Willingness to follow God's lead

(1) (2) (3) (4) (5)

WORD CHECK
Applying Scripture to life.

(1) (2) (3) (4) (5)

EQUIPPING GOALS

Who am I training or coaching this week? (Moving from doing everything to equipping everyone)

RESPONSIVE MARGIN

How much "white space" have I left in my schedule to weep with those who weep?

Limits and Boundaries

PRIORITIES THIS WEEK (TOP 3)

Focus on predicable rhythmns like sermon prep or startegic thinking.

1

2

3

SECONDARY NEEDS

Tasks that are importnat but not primary.

ITEMS TO DISCUSS WITH A MENTOR

Challenges, Dark Side patterns or relations isolation.

THE ART OF SAYING "NO."

Which digital limits or non-essential requests will I decline to protect my family and soul?

Reflections and Joy

CULTIVATING JOY: 3 ITEMS FOR GRATITUDE

Gratitude guards the heart and restores perspective

1

2

3

GENERAL REFLECTION

Frre-form thoughts, shenanigans, and wound of ministry

INTEGRATION QUESTION

What small adjustment this week moved me toward mental and emotional health?

Soul Health

DATE(S) [   ]

SCRIPTURE MEMORY
Focus verse for this week

WORSHIP REFLECTION

How did I practice "often and solitary" time with the Father?

PRAYERS FOR YOUR PEOPLE

The flock entrusted to you.

PRAYERS FOR MY FAMILY

Spouse, children and grandchildren

PRAYERS FOR MYSELF

Personal burdens and requests

Rhythms and Renewal

BURNOUT DANGER LEVEL

Where am I on the road to burnout today?

DAILY RHYTHM CHECK

EXERCISE TODAY?
☐ YES ☐ NO

SPIRITUAL GIFTS PRIMARY?
☐ YES ☐ NO

HEALTHY EATING TODAY?
☐ YES ☐ NO

RESTORATIVE SLEEP?
☐ YES ☐ NO

SABBATH RHYTHM and RENEWAL

What "Protected Space" will I Safeguard this week?

PROCESSING CRITICISM

Discern truth, release falsehood, stay anchored in God's approval.

Formed for Ministry

PROCESS ITEMS CHECK

Rate how God is testing you this week (1-5 scale)

INTEGRITY CHECK
Character Consistency

(1) (2) (3) (4) (5)

OBEDIENCE CHECK
Willingness to follow God's lead

(1) (2) (3) (4) (5)

WORD CHECK
Applying Scripture to life.

(1) (2) (3) (4) (5)

EQUIPPING GOALS

Who am I training or coaching this week? (Moving from doing everything to equipping everyone)

RESPONSIVE MARGIN

How much "white space" have I left in my schedule to weep with those who weep?

Limits and Boundaries

PRIORITIES THIS WEEK (TOP 3)

Focus on predicable rhythmns like sermon prep or startegic thinking.

1

2

3

SECONDARY NEEDS

Tasks that are importnat but not primary.

ITEMS TO DISCUSS WITH A MENTOR

Challenges, Dark Side patterns or relations isolation.

THE ART OF SAYING "NO."

Which digital limits or non-essential requests will I decline to protect my family and soul?

Reflections and Joy

CULTIVATING JOY: 3 ITEMS FOR GRATITUDE

Gratitude guards the heart and restores perspective

1

2

3

GENERAL REFLECTION

Frre-form thoughts, shenanigans, and wound of ministry

INTEGRATION QUESTION

What small adjustment this week moved me toward mental and emotional health?

Soul Health

DATE(S)

SCRIPTURE MEMORY
Focus verse for this week

WORSHIP REFLECTION

How did I practice "often and solitary" time with the Father?

PRAYERS FOR YOUR PEOPLE

The flock entrusted to you.

PRAYERS FOR MY FAMILY

Spouse, children and grandchildren

PRAYERS FOR MYSELF

Personal burdens and requests

Rhythms and Renewal

BURNOUT DANGER LEVEL

Where am I on the road to burnout today?

DAILY RHYTHM CHECK

EXERCISE TODAY?

☐ YES ☐ NO

SPIRITUAL GIFTS PRIMARY?

☐ YES ☐ NO

HEALTHY EATING TODAY?

☐ YES ☐ NO

RESTORATIVE SLEEP?

☐ YES ☐ NO

SABBATH RHYTHM and RENEWAL

What "Protected Space" will I Safeguard this week?

PROCESSING CRITICISM

Discern truth, release falsehood, stay anchored in God's approval.

Formed for Ministry

PROCESS ITEMS CHECK

Rate how God is testing you this week (1-5 scale)

INTEGRITY CHECK
Character Consistency

(1)   (2)   (3)   (4)   (5)

OBEDIENCE CHECK
Willingness to follow God's lead

(1)   (2)   (3)   (4)   (5)

WORD CHECK
Applying Scripture to life.

(1)   (2)   (3)   (4)   (5)

EQUIPPING GOALS

Who am I training or coaching this week? (Moving from doing everything to equipping everyone)

RESPONSIVE MARGIN

How much "white space" have I left in my schedule to weep with those who weep?

Limits and Boundaries

PRIORITIES THIS WEEK (TOP 3)

Focus on predicable rhythmns like sermon prep or startegic thinking.

1

2

3

SECONDARY NEEDS

Tasks that are importnat but not primary.

ITEMS TO DISCUSS WITH A MENTOR

Challenges, Dark Side patterns or relations isolation.

THE ART OF SAYING "NO."

Which digital limits or non-essential requests will I decline to protect my family and soul?

Reflections and Joy

CULTIVATING JOY: 3 ITEMS FOR GRATITUDE

Gratitude guards the heart and restores perspective

1

2

3

GENERAL REFLECTION

Frre-form thoughts, shenanigans, and wound of ministry

INTEGRATION QUESTION

What small adjustment this week moved me toward mental and emotional health?

Soul Health

DATE(S)

SCRIPTURE MEMORY
Focus verse for this week

WORSHIP REFLECTION
How did I practice "often and solitary" time with the Father?

PRAYERS FOR YOUR PEOPLE
The flock entrusted to you.

PRAYERS FOR MY FAMILY
Spouse, children and grandchildren

PRAYERS FOR MYSELF
Personal burdens and requests

Rhythms and Renewal

BURNOUT DANGER LEVEL

Where am I on the road to burnout today?

DAILY RHYTHM CHECK

EXERCISE TODAY?

☐ YES ☐ NO

SPIRITUAL GIFTS PRIMARY?

☐ YES ☐ NO

HEALTHY EATING TODAY?

☐ YES ☐ NO

RESTORATIVE SLEEP?

☐ YES ☐ NO

SABBATH RHYTHM and RENEWAL

What "Protected Space" will I Safeguard this week?

PROCESSING CRITICISM

Discern truth, release falsehood, stay anchored in God's approval.

Formed for Ministry

PROCESS ITEMS CHECK

Rate how God is testing you this week (1-5 scale)

INTEGRITY CHECK
Character Consistency

(1) (2) (3) (4) (5)

OBEDIENCE CHECK
Willingness to follow God's lead

(1) (2) (3) (4) (5)

WORD CHECK
Applying Scripture to life.

(1) (2) (3) (4) (5)

EQUIPPING GOALS

Who am I training or coaching this week? (Moving from doing everything to equipping everyone)

RESPONSIVE MARGIN

How much "white space" have I left in my schedule to weep with those who weep?

Limits and Boundaries

PRIORITIES THIS WEEK (TOP 3)

Focus on predicable rhythmns like sermon prep or startegic thinking.

1

2

3

SECONDARY NEEDS

Tasks that are importnat but not primary.

ITEMS TO DISCUSS WITH A MENTOR

Challenges, Dark Side patterns or relations isolation.

THE ART OF SAYING "NO."

Which digital limits or non-essential requests will I decline to protect my family and soul?

Reflections and Joy

CULTIVATING JOY: 3 ITEMS FOR GRATITUDE

Gratitude guards the heart and restores perspective

1

2

3

GENERAL REFLECTION

Frre-form thoughts, shenanigans, and wound of ministry

INTEGRATION QUESTION

What small adjustment this week moved me toward mental and emotional health?

Soul Health

DATE(S)

SCRIPTURE MEMORY
Focus verse for this week

WORSHIP REFLECTION

How did I practice "often and solitary" time with the Father?

PRAYERS FOR YOUR PEOPLE

The flock entrusted to you.

PRAYERS FOR MY FAMILY

Spouse, children and grandchildren

PRAYERS FOR MYSELF

Personal burdens and requests

Rhythms and Renewal

BURNOUT DANGER LEVEL

Where am I on the road to burnout today?

DAILY RHYTHM CHECK

EXERCISE TODAY?

☐ YES ☐ NO

SPIRITUAL GIFTS PRIMARY?

☐ YES ☐ NO

HEALTHY EATING TODAY?

☐ YES ☐ NO

RESTORATIVE SLEEP?

☐ YES ☐ NO

SABBATH RHYTHM and RENEWAL

What "Protected Space" will I Safeguard this week?

PROCESSING CRITICISM

Discern truth, release falsehood, stay anchored in God's approval.

Formed for Ministry

PROCESS ITEMS CHECK

Rate how God is testing you this week (1-5 scale)

INTEGRITY CHECK
Character Consistency

(1)   (2)   (3)   (4)   (5)

OBEDIENCE CHECK
Willingness to follow God's lead

(1)   (2)   (3)   (4)   (5)

WORD CHECK
Applying Scripture to life.

(1)   (2)   (3)   (4)   (5)

EQUIPPING GOALS

Who am I training or coaching this week? (Moving from doing everything to equipping everyone)

RESPONSIVE MARGIN

How much "white space" have I left in my schedule to weep with those who weep?

Limits and Boundaries

PRIORITIES THIS WEEK (TOP 3)

Focus on predicable rhythmns like sermon prep or startegic thinking.

1

2

3

SECONDARY NEEDS

Tasks that are importnat but not primary.

ITEMS TO DISCUSS WITH A MENTOR

Challenges, Dark Side patterns or relations isolation.

THE ART OF SAYING "NO."

Which digital limits or non-essential requests will I decline to protect my family and soul?

Reflections and Joy

CULTIVATING JOY: 3 ITEMS FOR GRATITUDE

Gratitude guards the heart and restores perspective

1

2

3

GENERAL REFLECTION

Frre-form thoughts, shenanigans, and wound of ministry

INTEGRATION QUESTION

What small adjustment this week moved me toward mental and emotional health?

Soul Health

DATE(S)

SCRIPTURE MEMORY
Focus verse for this week

WORSHIP REFLECTION

How did I practice "often and solitary" time with the Father?

PRAYERS FOR YOUR PEOPLE

The flock entrusted to you.

PRAYERS FOR MY FAMILY

Spouse, children and grandchildren

PRAYERS FOR MYSELF

Personal burdens and requests

Rhythms and Renewal

BURNOUT DANGER LEVEL

Where am I on the road to burnout today?

DAILY RHYTHM CHECK

EXERCISE TODAY?
☐ YES ☐ NO

SPIRITUAL GIFTS PRIMARY?
☐ YES ☐ NO

HEALTHY EATING TODAY?
☐ YES ☐ NO

RESTORATIVE SLEEP?
☐ YES ☐ NO

SABBATH RHYTHM and RENEWAL

What "Protected Space" will I Safeguard this week?

PROCESSING CRITICISM

Discern truth, release falsehood, stay anchored in God's approval.

Formed for Ministry

PROCESS ITEMS CHECK

Rate how God is testing you this week (1-5 scale)

INTEGRITY CHECK
Character Consistency

(1)   (2)   (3)   (4)   (5)

OBEDIENCE CHECK
Willingness to follow God's lead

(1)   (2)   (3)   (4)   (5)

WORD CHECK
Applying Scripture to life.

(1)   (2)   (3)   (4)   (5)

EQUIPPING GOALS

Who am I training or coaching this week? (Moving from doing everything to equipping everyone)

RESPONSIVE MARGIN

How much "white space" have I left in my schedule to weep with those who weep?

Limits and Boundaries

PRIORITIES THIS WEEK (TOP 3)

Focus on predicable rhythmns like sermon prep or startegic thinking.

1

2

3

SECONDARY NEEDS

Tasks that are importnat but not primary.

ITEMS TO DISCUSS WITH A MENTOR

Challenges, Dark Side patterns or relations isolation.

THE ART OF SAYING "NO."

Which digital limits or non-essential requests will I decline to protect my family and soul?

Reflections and Joy

CULTIVATING JOY: 3 ITEMS FOR GRATITUDE

Gratitude guards the heart and restores perspective

1

2

3

GENERAL REFLECTION

Frre-form thoughts, shenanigans, and wound of ministry

INTEGRATION QUESTION

What small adjustment this week moved me toward mental and emotional health?

Soul Health

DATE(S)

SCRIPTURE MEMORY
Focus verse for this week

WORSHIP REFLECTION

How did I practice "often and solitary" time with the Father?

PRAYERS FOR YOUR PEOPLE

The flock entrusted to you.

PRAYERS FOR MY FAMILY

Spouse, children and grandchildren

PRAYERS FOR MYSELF

Personal burdens and requests

Rhythms and Renewal

BURNOUT DANGER LEVEL

Where am I on the road to burnout today?

DAILY RHYTHM CHECK

EXERCISE TODAY?

☐ YES ☐ NO

SPIRITUAL GIFTS PRIMARY?

☐ YES ☐ NO

HEALTHY EATING TODAY?

☐ YES ☐ NO

RESTORATIVE SLEEP?

☐ YES ☐ NO

SABBATH RHYTHM and RENEWAL

What "Protected Space" will I Safeguard this week?

PROCESSING CRITICISM

Discern truth, release falsehood, stay anchored in God's approval.

Formed for Ministry

PROCESS ITEMS CHECK

Rate how God is testing you this week (1-5 scale)

INTEGRITY CHECK
Character Consistency

(1)   (2)   (3)   (4)   (5)

OBEDIENCE CHECK
Willingness to follow God's lead

(1)   (2)   (3)   (4)   (5)

WORD CHECK
Applying Scripture to life.

(1)   (2)   (3)   (4)   (5)

EQUIPPING GOALS

Who am I training or coaching this week? (Moving from doing everything to equipping everyone)

RESPONSIVE MARGIN

How much "white space" have I left in my schedule to weep with those who weep?

Limits and Boundaries

PRIORITIES THIS WEEK (TOP 3)

Focus on predicable rhythmns like sermon prep or startegic thinking.

1

2

3

SECONDARY NEEDS

Tasks that are importnat but not primary.

ITEMS TO DISCUSS WITH A MENTOR

Challenges, Dark Side patterns or relations isolation.

THE ART OF SAYING "NO."

Which digital limits or non-essential requests will I decline to protect my family and soul?

Reflections and Joy

CULTIVATING JOY: 3 ITEMS FOR GRATITUDE

Gratitude guards the heart and restores perspective

1

2

3

GENERAL REFLECTION

Frre-form thoughts, shenanigans, and wound of ministry

INTEGRATION QUESTION

What small adjustment this week moved me toward mental and emotional health?

DATE(S)

SCRIPTURE MEMORY
Focus verse for this week

WORSHIP REFLECTION
How did I practice "often and solitary" time with the Father?

PRAYERS FOR YOUR PEOPLE
The flock entrusted to you.

PRAYERS FOR MY FAMILY
Spouse, children and grandchildren

PRAYERS FOR MYSELF
Personal burdens and requests

Rhythms and Renewal

BURNOUT DANGER LEVEL

Where am I on the road to burnout today?

DAILY RHYTHM CHECK

EXERCISE TODAY?

☐ YES ☐ NO

HEALTHY EATING TODAY?

☐ YES ☐ NO

SPIRITUAL GIFTS PRIMARY?

☐ YES ☐ NO

RESTORATIVE SLEEP?

☐ YES ☐ NO

SABBATH RHYTHM and RENEWAL

What "Protected Space" will I Safeguard this week?

PROCESSING CRITICISM

Discern truth, release falsehood, stay anchored in God's approval.

Formed for Ministry

PROCESS ITEMS CHECK

Rate how God is testing you this week (1-5 scale)

INTEGRITY CHECK
Character Consistency

(1)   (2)   (3)   (4)   (5)

OBEDIENCE CHECK
Willingness to follow God's lead

(1)   (2)   (3)   (4)   (5)

WORD CHECK
Applying Scripture to life.

(1)   (2)   (3)   (4)   (5)

EQUIPPING GOALS

Who am I training or coaching this week? (Moving from doing everything to equipping everyone)

RESPONSIVE MARGIN

How much "white space" have I left in my schedule to weep with those who weep?

Limits and Boundaries

PRIORITIES THIS WEEK (TOP 3)

Focus on predicable rhythmns like sermon prep or startegic thinking.

1

2

3

SECONDARY NEEDS

Tasks that are importnat but not primary.

ITEMS TO DISCUSS WITH A MENTOR

Challenges, Dark Side patterns or relations isolation.

THE ART OF SAYING "NO."

Which digital limits or non-essential requests will I decline to protect my family and soul?

Reflections and Joy

CULTIVATING JOY: 3 ITEMS FOR GRATITUDE

Gratitude guards the heart and restores perspective

1

2

3

GENERAL REFLECTION

Frre-form thoughts, shenanigans, and wound of ministry

INTEGRATION QUESTION

What small adjustment this week moved me toward mental and emotional health?

Soul Health

SCRIPTURE MEMORY
Focus verse for this week

WORSHIP REFLECTION

How did I practice "often and solitary" time with the Father?

PRAYERS FOR YOUR PEOPLE

The flock entrusted to you.

PRAYERS FOR MY FAMILY

Spouse, children and grandchildren

PRAYERS FOR MYSELF

Personal burdens and requests

Rhythms and Renewal

BURNOUT DANGER LEVEL

Where am I on the road to burnout today?

DAILY RHYTHM CHECK

EXERCISE TODAY?

☐ YES ☐ NO

SPIRITUAL GIFTS PRIMARY?

☐ YES ☐ NO

HEALTHY EATING TODAY?

☐ YES ☐ NO

RESTORATIVE SLEEP?

☐ YES ☐ NO

SABBATH RHYTHM and RENEWAL

What "Protected Space" will I Safeguard this week?

PROCESSING CRITICISM

Discern truth, release falsehood, stay anchored in God's approval.

Formed for Ministry

PROCESS ITEMS CHECK

Rate how God is testing you this week (1-5 scale)

INTEGRITY CHECK
Character Consistency

(1) (2) (3) (4) (5)

OBEDIENCE CHECK
Willingness to follow God's lead

(1) (2) (3) (4) (5)

WORD CHECK
Applying Scripture to life.

(1) (2) (3) (4) (5)

EQUIPPING GOALS

Who am I training or coaching this week? (Moving from doing everything to equipping everyone)

RESPONSIVE MARGIN

How much "white space" have I left in my schedule to weep with those who weep?

Limits and Boundaries

PRIORITIES THIS WEEK (TOP 3)

Focus on predicable rhythmns like sermon prep or startegic thinking.

1

2

3

SECONDARY NEEDS

Tasks that are importnat but not primary.

ITEMS TO DISCUSS WITH A MENTOR

Challenges, Dark Side patterns or relations isolation.

THE ART OF SAYING "NO."

Which digital limits or non-essential requests will I decline to protect my family and soul?

Reflections and Joy

CULTIVATING JOY: 3 ITEMS FOR GRATITUDE

Gratitude guards the heart and restores perspective

1

2

3

GENERAL REFLECTION

Frre-form thoughts, shenanigans, and wound of ministry

INTEGRATION QUESTION

What small adjustment this week moved me toward mental and emotional health?

Soul Health

DATE(S)

SCRIPTURE MEMORY
Focus verse for this week

WORSHIP REFLECTION

How did I practice "often and solitary" time with the Father?

PRAYERS FOR YOUR PEOPLE

The flock entrusted to you.

PRAYERS FOR MY FAMILY

Spouse, children and grandchildren

PRAYERS FOR MYSELF

Personal burdens and requests

Rhythms and Renewal

BURNOUT DANGER LEVEL

Where am I on the road to burnout today?

DAILY RHYTHM CHECK

EXERCISE TODAY?
☐ YES ☐ NO

SPIRITUAL GIFTS PRIMARY?
☐ YES ☐ NO

HEALTHY EATING TODAY?
☐ YES ☐ NO

RESTORATIVE SLEEP?
☐ YES ☐ NO

SABBATH RHYTHM and RENEWAL

What "Protected Space" will I Safeguard this week?

PROCESSING CRITICISM

Discern truth, release falsehood, stay anchored in God's approval.

Formed for Ministry

PROCESS ITEMS CHECK

Rate how God is testing you this week (1-5 scale)

INTEGRITY CHECK
Character Consistency

(1) (2) (3) (4) (5)

OBEDIENCE CHECK
Willingness to follow God's lead

(1) (2) (3) (4) (5)

WORD CHECK
Applying Scripture to life.

(1) (2) (3) (4) (5)

EQUIPPING GOALS

Who am I training or coaching this week? (Moving from doing everything to equipping everyone)

RESPONSIVE MARGIN

How much "white space" have I left in my schedule to weep with those who weep?

Limits and Boundaries

PRIORITIES THIS WEEK (TOP 3)

Focus on predicable rhythmns like sermon prep or startegic thinking.

1

2

3

SECONDARY NEEDS

Tasks that are importnat but not primary.

ITEMS TO DISCUSS WITH A MENTOR

Challenges, Dark Side patterns or relations isolation.

THE ART OF SAYING "NO."

Which digital limits or non-essential requests will I decline to protect my family and soul?

Reflections and Joy

CULTIVATING JOY: 3 ITEMS FOR GRATITUDE

Gratitude guards the heart and restores perspective

1

2

3

GENERAL REFLECTION

Frre-form thoughts, shenanigans, and wound of ministry

INTEGRATION QUESTION

What small adjustment this week moved me toward mental and emotional health?

Soul Health

DATE(S)

SCRIPTURE MEMORY
Focus verse for this week

WORSHIP REFLECTION

How did I practice "often and solitary" time with the Father?

PRAYERS FOR YOUR PEOPLE

The flock entrusted to you.

PRAYERS FOR MY FAMILY

Spouse, children and grandchildren

PRAYERS FOR MYSELF

Personal burdens and requests

Rhythms and Renewal

BURNOUT DANGER LEVEL

Where am I on the road to burnout today?

DAILY RHYTHM CHECK

EXERCISE TODAY?

☐ YES ☐ NO

SPIRITUAL GIFTS PRIMARY?

☐ YES ☐ NO

HEALTHY EATING TODAY?

☐ YES ☐ NO

RESTORATIVE SLEEP?

☐ YES ☐ NO

SABBATH RHYTHM and RENEWAL

What "Protected Space" will I Safeguard this week?

PROCESSING CRITICISM

Discern truth, release falsehood, stay anchored in God's approval.

Formed for Ministry

PROCESS ITEMS CHECK

Rate how God is testing you this week (1-5 scale)

INTEGRITY CHECK
Character Consistency

(1)   (2)   (3)   (4)   (5)

OBEDIENCE CHECK
Willingness to follow God's lead

(1)   (2)   (3)   (4)   (5)

WORD CHECK
Applying Scripture to life.

(1)   (2)   (3)   (4)   (5)

EQUIPPING GOALS

Who am I training or coaching this week? (Moving from doing everything to equipping everyone)

RESPONSIVE MARGIN

How much "white space" have I left in my schedule to weep with those who weep?

Limits and Boundaries

PRIORITIES THIS WEEK (TOP 3)

Focus on predicable rhythmns like sermon prep or startegic thinking.

1

2

3

SECONDARY NEEDS

Tasks that are importnat but not primary.

ITEMS TO DISCUSS WITH A MENTOR

Challenges, Dark Side patterns or relations isolation.

THE ART OF SAYING "NO."

Which digital limits or non-essential requests will I decline to protect my family and soul?

Reflections and Joy

CULTIVATING JOY: 3 ITEMS FOR GRATITUDE

Gratitude guards the heart and restores perspective

1

2

3

GENERAL REFLECTION

Frre-form thoughts, shenanigans, and wound of ministry

INTEGRATION QUESTION

What small adjustment this week moved me toward mental and emotional health?

Soul Health

DATE(S)

SCRIPTURE MEMORY
Focus verse for this week

WORSHIP REFLECTION

How did I practice "often and solitary" time with the Father?

PRAYERS FOR YOUR PEOPLE

The flock entrusted to you.

PRAYERS FOR MY FAMILY

Spouse, children and grandchildren

PRAYERS FOR MYSELF

Personal burdens and requests

Rhythms and Renewal

BURNOUT DANGER LEVEL

Where am I on the road to burnout today?

DAILY RHYTHM CHECK

EXERCISE TODAY?

☐ YES ☐ NO

SPIRITUAL GIFTS PRIMARY?

☐ YES ☐ NO

HEALTHY EATING TODAY?

☐ YES ☐ NO

RESTORATIVE SLEEP?

☐ YES ☐ NO

SABBATH RHYTHM and RENEWAL

What "Protected Space" will I Safeguard this week?

PROCESSING CRITICISM

Discern truth, release falsehood, stay anchored in God's approval.

Formed for Ministry

PROCESS ITEMS CHECK

Rate how God is testing you this week (1-5 scale)

INTEGRITY CHECK
Character Consistency

(1) (2) (3) (4) (5)

OBEDIENCE CHECK
Willingness to follow God's lead

(1) (2) (3) (4) (5)

WORD CHECK
Applying Scripture to life.

(1) (2) (3) (4) (5)

EQUIPPING GOALS

Who am I training or coaching this week? (Moving from doing everything to equipping everyone)

RESPONSIVE MARGIN

How much "white space" have I left in my schedule to weep with those who weep?

Limits and Boundaries

PRIORITIES THIS WEEK (TOP 3)

Focus on predicable rhythmns like sermon prep or startegic thinking.

1

2

3

SECONDARY NEEDS

Tasks that are importnat but not primary.

ITEMS TO DISCUSS WITH A MENTOR

Challenges, Dark Side patterns or relations isolation.

THE ART OF SAYING "NO."

Which digital limits or non-essential requests will I decline to protect my family and soul?

Reflections and Joy

CULTIVATING JOY: 3 ITEMS FOR GRATITUDE

Gratitude guards the heart and restores perspective

1

2

3

GENERAL REFLECTION

Frre-form thoughts, shenanigans, and wound of ministry

INTEGRATION QUESTION

What small adjustment this week moved me toward mental and emotional health?

Soul Health

DATE(S)

SCRIPTURE MEMORY
Focus verse for this week

WORSHIP REFLECTION

How did I practice "often and solitary" time with the Father?

PRAYERS FOR YOUR PEOPLE

The flock entrusted to you.

PRAYERS FOR MY FAMILY

Spouse, children and grandchildren

PRAYERS FOR MYSELF

Personal burdens and requests

Rhythms and Renewal

BURNOUT DANGER LEVEL

Where am I on the road to burnout today?

DAILY RHYTHM CHECK

EXERCISE TODAY?

☐ YES ☐ NO

HEALTHY EATING TODAY?

☐ YES ☐ NO

SPIRITUAL GIFTS PRIMARY?

☐ YES ☐ NO

RESTORATIVE SLEEP?

☐ YES ☐ NO

SABBATH RHYTHM and RENEWAL

What "Protected Space" will I Safeguard this week?

PROCESSING CRITICISM

Discern truth, release falsehood, stay anchored in God's approval.

Formed for Ministry

PROCESS ITEMS CHECK

Rate how God is testing you this week (1-5 scale)

INTEGRITY CHECK
Character Consistency

(1) (2) (3) (4) (5)

OBEDIENCE CHECK
Willingness to follow God's lead

(1) (2) (3) (4) (5)

WORD CHECK
Applying Scripture to life.

(1) (2) (3) (4) (5)

EQUIPPING GOALS

Who am I training or coaching this week? (Moving from doing everything to equipping everyone)

RESPONSIVE MARGIN

How much "white space" have I left in my schedule to weep with those who weep?

Limits and Boundaries

PRIORITIES THIS WEEK (TOP 3)

Focus on predicable rhythmns like sermon prep or startegic thinking.

1

2

3

SECONDARY NEEDS

Tasks that are importnat but not primary.

ITEMS TO DISCUSS WITH A MENTOR

Challenges, Dark Side patterns or relations isolation.

THE ART OF SAYING "NO."

Which digital limits or non-essential requests will I decline to protect my family and soul?

Reflections and Joy

CULTIVATING JOY: 3 ITEMS FOR GRATITUDE

Gratitude guards the heart and restores perspective

1

2

3

GENERAL REFLECTION

Frre-form thoughts, shenanigans, and wound of ministry

INTEGRATION QUESTION

What small adjustment this week moved me toward mental and emotional health?

Soul Health

DATE(S)

SCRIPTURE MEMORY
Focus verse for this week

WORSHIP REFLECTION

How did I practice "often and solitary" time with the Father?

PRAYERS FOR YOUR PEOPLE

The flock entrusted to you.

PRAYERS FOR MY FAMILY

Spouse, children and grandchildren

PRAYERS FOR MYSELF

Personal burdens and requests

Rhythms and Renewal

BURNOUT DANGER LEVEL

Where am I on the road to burnout today?

DAILY RHYTHM CHECK

EXERCISE TODAY?
☐ YES ☐ NO

SPIRITUAL GIFTS PRIMARY?
☐ YES ☐ NO

HEALTHY EATING TODAY?
☐ YES ☐ NO

RESTORATIVE SLEEP?
☐ YES ☐ NO

SABBATH RHYTHM and RENEWAL

What "Protected Space" will I Safeguard this week?

PROCESSING CRITICISM

Discern truth, release falsehood, stay anchored in God's approval.

Formed for Ministry

PROCESS ITEMS CHECK

Rate how God is testing you this week (1-5 scale)

INTEGRITY CHECK
Character Consistency

① ② ③ ④ ⑤

OBEDIENCE CHECK
Willingness to follow God's lead

① ② ③ ④ ⑤

WORD CHECK
Applying Scripture to life.

① ② ③ ④ ⑤

EQUIPPING GOALS

Who am I training or coaching this week? (Moving from doing everything to equipping everyone)

RESPONSIVE MARGIN

How much "white space" have I left in my schedule to weep with those who weep?

Limits and Boundaries

PRIORITIES THIS WEEK (TOP 3)

Focus on predicable rhythmns like sermon prep or startegic thinking.

1

2

3

SECONDARY NEEDS

Tasks that are importnat but not primary.

ITEMS TO DISCUSS WITH A MENTOR

Challenges, Dark Side patterns or relations isolation.

THE ART OF SAYING "NO."

Which digital limits or non-essential requests will I decline to protect my family and soul?

Reflections and Joy

CULTIVATING JOY: 3 ITEMS FOR GRATITUDE

Gratitude guards the heart and restores perspective

1

2

3

GENERAL REFLECTION

Frre-form thoughts, shenanigans, and wound of ministry

INTEGRATION QUESTION

What small adjustment this week moved me toward mental and emotional health?

DATE(S) [   ]

SCRIPTURE MEMORY
Focus verse for this week

WORSHIP REFLECTION

How did I practice "often and solitary" time with the Father?

PRAYERS FOR YOUR PEOPLE

The flock entrusted to you.

PRAYERS FOR MY FAMILY

Spouse, children and grandchildren

PRAYERS FOR MYSELF

Personal burdens and requests

Rhythms and Renewal

BURNOUT DANGER LEVEL

Where am I on the road to burnout today?

| 1 | 2 | 3 | 4 | 5 | 6 | 7 | 8 | 9 | 10 |

DAILY RHYTHM CHECK

EXERCISE TODAY?
☐ YES ☐ NO

SPIRITUAL GIFTS PRIMARY?
☐ YES ☐ NO

HEALTHY EATING TODAY?
☐ YES ☐ NO

RESTORATIVE SLEEP?
☐ YES ☐ NO

SABBATH RHYTHM and RENEWAL

What "Protected Space" will I Safeguard this week?

PROCESSING CRITICISM

Discern truth, release falsehood, stay anchored in God's approval.

Formed for Ministry

PROCESS ITEMS CHECK

Rate how God is testing you this week (1-5 scale)

INTEGRITY CHECK
Character Consistency

(1)　(2)　(3)　(4)　(5)

OBEDIENCE CHECK
Willingness to follow God's lead

(1)　(2)　(3)　(4)　(5)

WORD CHECK
Applying Scripture to life.

(1)　(2)　(3)　(4)　(5)

EQUIPPING GOALS

Who am I training or coaching this week? (Moving from doing everything to equipping everyone)

RESPONSIVE MARGIN

How much "white space" have I left in my schedule to weep with those who weep?

Limits and Boundaries

PRIORITIES THIS WEEK (TOP 3)

Focus on predicable rhythmns like sermon prep or startegic thinking.

1

2

3

SECONDARY NEEDS

Tasks that are importnat but not primary.

ITEMS TO DISCUSS WITH A MENTOR

Challenges, Dark Side patterns or relations isolation.

THE ART OF SAYING "NO."

Which digital limits or non-essential requests will I decline to protect my family and soul?

Reflections and Joy

CULTIVATING JOY: 3 ITEMS FOR GRATITUDE

Gratitude guards the heart and restores perspective

1

2

3

GENERAL REFLECTION

Frre-form thoughts, shenanigans, and wound of ministry

INTEGRATION QUESTION

What small adjustment this week moved me toward mental and emotional health?

Soul Health

DATE(S)

SCRIPTURE MEMORY
Focus verse for this week

WORSHIP REFLECTION

How did I practice "often and solitary" time with the Father?

PRAYERS FOR YOUR PEOPLE

The flock entrusted to you.

PRAYERS FOR MY FAMILY

Spouse, children and grandchildren

PRAYERS FOR MYSELF

Personal burdens and requests

Rhythms and Renewal

BURNOUT DANGER LEVEL

Where am I on the road to burnout today?

| 0 | 1 | 2 | 3 | 4 | 5 | 6 | 7 | 8 | 9 | 10 |

DAILY RHYTHM CHECK

EXERCISE TODAY?
☐ YES ☐ NO

SPIRITUAL GIFTS PRIMARY?
☐ YES ☐ NO

HEALTHY EATING TODAY?
☐ YES ☐ NO

RESTORATIVE SLEEP?
☐ YES ☐ NO

SABBATH RHYTHM and RENEWAL

What "Protected Space" will I Safeguard this week?

PROCESSING CRITICISM

Discern truth, release falsehood, stay anchored in God's approval.

Formed for Ministry

PROCESS ITEMS CHECK

Rate how God is testing you this week (1-5 scale)

INTEGRITY CHECK
Character Consistency

(1)　(2)　(3)　(4)　(5)

OBEDIENCE CHECK
Willingness to follow God's lead

(1)　(2)　(3)　(4)　(5)

WORD CHECK
Applying Scripture to life.

(1)　(2)　(3)　(4)　(5)

EQUIPPING GOALS

Who am I training or coaching this week? (Moving from doing everything to equipping everyone)

RESPONSIVE MARGIN

How much "white space" have I left in my schedule to weep with those who weep?

Limits and Boundaries

PRIORITIES THIS WEEK (TOP 3)

Focus on predicable rhythmns like sermon prep or startegic thinking.

1

2

3

SECONDARY NEEDS

Tasks that are importnat but not primary.

ITEMS TO DISCUSS WITH A MENTOR

Challenges, Dark Side patterns or relations isolation.

THE ART OF SAYING "NO."

Which digital limits or non-essential requests will I decline to protect my family and soul?

Reflections and Joy

CULTIVATING JOY: 3 ITEMS FOR GRATITUDE

Gratitude guards the heart and restores perspective

1

2

3

GENERAL REFLECTION

Frre-form thoughts, shenanigans, and wound of ministry

INTEGRATION QUESTION

What small adjustment this week moved me toward mental and emotional health?

DATE(S)

SCRIPTURE MEMORY
Focus verse for this week

WORSHIP REFLECTION

How did I practice "often and solitary" time with the Father?

PRAYERS FOR YOUR PEOPLE

The flock entrusted to you.

PRAYERS FOR MY FAMILY

Spouse, children and grandchildren

PRAYERS FOR MYSELF

Personal burdens and requests

Rhythms and Renewal

BURNOUT DANGER LEVEL

Where am I on the road to burnout today?

DAILY RHYTHM CHECK

EXERCISE TODAY?

[ ] YES [ ] NO

HEALTHY EATING TODAY?

[ ] YES [ ] NO

SPIRITUAL GIFTS PRIMARY?

[ ] YES [ ] NO

RESTORATIVE SLEEP?

[ ] YES [ ] NO

SABBATH RHYTHM and RENEWAL

What "Protected Space" will I Safeguard this week?

PROCESSING CRITICISM

Discern truth, release falsehood, stay anchored in God's approval.

Formed for Ministry

PROCESS ITEMS CHECK

Rate how God is testing you this week (1-5 scale)

INTEGRITY CHECK
Character Consistency
① ② ③ ④ ⑤

OBEDIENCE CHECK
Willingness to follow God's lead
① ② ③ ④ ⑤

WORD CHECK
Applying Scripture to life.
① ② ③ ④ ⑤

EQUIPPING GOALS

Who am I training or coaching this week? (Moving from doing everything to equipping everyone)

RESPONSIVE MARGIN

How much "white space" have I left in my schedule to weep with those who weep?

Limits and Boundaries

PRIORITIES THIS WEEK (TOP 3)

Focus on predicable rhythmns like sermon prep or startegic thinking.

1

2

3

SECONDARY NEEDS

Tasks that are importnat but not primary.

ITEMS TO DISCUSS WITH A MENTOR

Challenges, Dark Side patterns or relations isolation.

THE ART OF SAYING "NO."

Which digital limits or non-essential requests will I decline to protect my family and soul?

Reflections and Joy

CULTIVATING JOY: 3 ITEMS FOR GRATITUDE

Gratitude guards the heart and restores perspective

1

2

3

GENERAL REFLECTION

Frre-form thoughts, shenanigans, and wound of ministry

INTEGRATION QUESTION

What small adjustment this week moved me toward mental and emotional health?

Soul Health

DATE(S)

SCRIPTURE MEMORY
Focus verse for this week

WORSHIP REFLECTION

How did I practice "often and solitary" time with the Father?

PRAYERS FOR YOUR PEOPLE

The flock entrusted to you.

PRAYERS FOR MY FAMILY

Spouse, children and grandchildren

PRAYERS FOR MYSELF

Personal burdens and requests

Rhythms and Renewal

BURNOUT DANGER LEVEL

Where am I on the road to burnout today?

DAILY RHYTHM CHECK

EXERCISE TODAY?

☐ YES ☐ NO

SPIRITUAL GIFTS PRIMARY?

☐ YES ☐ NO

HEALTHY EATING TODAY?

☐ YES ☐ NO

RESTORATIVE SLEEP?

☐ YES ☐ NO

SABBATH RHYTHM and RENEWAL

What "Protected Space" will I Safeguard this week?

PROCESSING CRITICISM

Discern truth, release falsehood, stay anchored in God's approval.

Formed for Ministry

PROCESS ITEMS CHECK

Rate how God is testing you this week (1-5 scale)

INTEGRITY CHECK
Character Consistency

(1) (2) (3) (4) (5)

OBEDIENCE CHECK
Willingness to follow God's lead

(1) (2) (3) (4) (5)

WORD CHECK
Applying Scripture to life.

(1) (2) (3) (4) (5)

EQUIPPING GOALS

Who am I training or coaching this week? (Moving from doing everything to equipping everyone)

RESPONSIVE MARGIN

How much "white space" have I left in my schedule to weep with those who weep?

Limits and Boundaries

PRIORITIES THIS WEEK (TOP 3)

Focus on predicable rhythmns like sermon prep or startegic thinking.

1

2

3

SECONDARY NEEDS

Tasks that are importnat but not primary.

ITEMS TO DISCUSS WITH A MENTOR

Challenges, Dark Side patterns or relations isolation.

THE ART OF SAYING "NO."

Which digital limits or non-essential requests will I decline to protect my family and soul?

Reflections and Joy

CULTIVATING JOY: 3 ITEMS FOR GRATITUDE

Gratitude guards the heart and restores perspective

1

2

3

GENERAL REFLECTION

Frre-form thoughts, shenanigans, and wound of ministry

INTEGRATION QUESTION

What small adjustment this week moved me toward mental and emotional health?

Soul Health

DATE(S)

SCRIPTURE MEMORY
Focus verse for this week

WORSHIP REFLECTION

How did I practice "often and solitary" time with the Father?

PRAYERS FOR YOUR PEOPLE

The flock entrusted to you.

PRAYERS FOR MY FAMILY

Spouse, children and grandchildren

PRAYERS FOR MYSELF

Personal burdens and requests

Rhythms and Renewal

BURNOUT DANGER LEVEL

Where am I on the road to burnout today?

DAILY RHYTHM CHECK

EXERCISE TODAY?

☐ YES ☐ NO

SPIRITUAL GIFTS PRIMARY?

☐ YES ☐ NO

HEALTHY EATING TODAY?

☐ YES ☐ NO

RESTORATIVE SLEEP?

☐ YES ☐ NO

SABBATH RHYTHM and RENEWAL

What "Protected Space" will I Safeguard this week?

PROCESSING CRITICISM

Discern truth, release falsehood, stay anchored in God's approval.

Formed for Ministry

PROCESS ITEMS CHECK

Rate how God is testing you this week (1-5 scale)

INTEGRITY CHECK
Character Consistency
(1) (2) (3) (4) (5)

OBEDIENCE CHECK
Willingness to follow God's lead
(1) (2) (3) (4) (5)

WORD CHECK
Applying Scripture to life.
(1) (2) (3) (4) (5)

EQUIPPING GOALS

Who am I training or coaching this week? (Moving from doing everything to equipping everyone)

RESPONSIVE MARGIN

How much "white space" have I left in my schedule to weep with those who weep?

Limits and Boundaries

PRIORITIES THIS WEEK (TOP 3)

Focus on predicable rhythmns like sermon prep or startegic thinking.

1

2

3

SECONDARY NEEDS

Tasks that are importnat but not primary.

ITEMS TO DISCUSS WITH A MENTOR

Challenges, Dark Side patterns or relations isolation.

THE ART OF SAYING "NO."

Which digital limits or non-essential requests will I decline to protect my family and soul?

Reflections and Joy

CULTIVATING JOY: 3 ITEMS FOR GRATITUDE

Gratitude guards the heart and restores perspective

1

2

3

GENERAL REFLECTION

Frre-form thoughts, shenanigans, and wound of ministry

INTEGRATION QUESTION

What small adjustment this week moved me toward mental and emotional health?

DATE(S) [ ]

SCRIPTURE MEMORY
Focus verse for this week

WORSHIP REFLECTION

How did I practice "often and solitary" time with the Father?

PRAYERS FOR YOUR PEOPLE

The flock entrusted to you.

PRAYERS FOR MY FAMILY

Spouse, children and grandchildren

PRAYERS FOR MYSELF

Personal burdens and requests

Rhythms and Renewal

BURNOUT DANGER LEVEL

Where am I on the road to burnout today?

DAILY RHYTHM CHECK

EXERCISE TODAY?
☐ YES ☐ NO

SPIRITUAL GIFTS PRIMARY?
☐ YES ☐ NO

HEALTHY EATING TODAY?
☐ YES ☐ NO

RESTORATIVE SLEEP?
☐ YES ☐ NO

SABBATH RHYTHM and RENEWAL

What "Protected Space" will I Safeguard this week?

PROCESSING CRITICISM

Discern truth, release falsehood, stay anchored in God's approval.

Formed for Ministry

PROCESS ITEMS CHECK

Rate how God is testing you this week (1-5 scale)

INTEGRITY CHECK
Character Consistency

(1) (2) (3) (4) (5)

OBEDIENCE CHECK
Willingness to follow God's lead

(1) (2) (3) (4) (5)

WORD CHECK
Applying Scripture to life.

(1) (2) (3) (4) (5)

EQUIPPING GOALS

Who am I training or coaching this week? (Moving from doing everything to equipping everyone)

RESPONSIVE MARGIN

How much "white space" have I left in my schedule to weep with those who weep?

Limits and Boundaries

PRIORITIES THIS WEEK (TOP 3)

Focus on predicable rhythmns like sermon prep or startegic thinking.

1

2

3

SECONDARY NEEDS

Tasks that are importnat but not primary.

ITEMS TO DISCUSS WITH A MENTOR

Challenges, Dark Side patterns or relations isolation.

THE ART OF SAYING "NO."

Which digital limits or non-essential requests will I decline to protect my family and soul?

Reflections and Joy

CULTIVATING JOY: 3 ITEMS FOR GRATITUDE

Gratitude guards the heart and restores perspective

1

2

3

GENERAL REFLECTION

Frre-form thoughts, shenanigans, and wound of ministry

INTEGRATION QUESTION

What small adjustment this week moved me toward mental and emotional health?

Soul Health

DATE(S) [   ]

SCRIPTURE MEMORY
Focus verse for this week

WORSHIP REFLECTION

How did I practice "often and solitary" time with the Father?

PRAYERS FOR YOUR PEOPLE

The flock entrusted to you.

PRAYERS FOR MY FAMILY

Spouse, children and grandchildren

PRAYERS FOR MYSELF

Personal burdens and requests

Rhythms and Renewal

BURNOUT DANGER LEVEL

Where am I on the road to burnout today?

DAILY RHYTHM CHECK

EXERCISE TODAY?

☐ YES ☐ NO

HEALTHY EATING TODAY?

☐ YES ☐ NO

SPIRITUAL GIFTS PRIMARY?

☐ YES ☐ NO

RESTORATIVE SLEEP?

☐ YES ☐ NO

SABBATH RHYTHM and RENEWAL

What "Protected Space" will I Safeguard this week?

PROCESSING CRITICISM

Discern truth, release falsehood, stay anchored in God's approval.

Formed for Ministry

PROCESS ITEMS CHECK

Rate how God is testing you this week (1-5 scale)

INTEGRITY CHECK
Character Consistency

(1)   (2)   (3)   (4)   (5)

OBEDIENCE CHECK
Willingness to follow God's lead

(1)   (2)   (3)   (4)   (5)

WORD CHECK
Applying Scripture to life.

(1)   (2)   (3)   (4)   (5)

EQUIPPING GOALS

Who am I training or coaching this week? (Moving from doing everything to equipping everyone)

RESPONSIVE MARGIN

How much "white space" have I left in my schedule to weep with those who weep?

Limits and Boundaries

PRIORITIES THIS WEEK (TOP 3)

Focus on predicable rhythmns like sermon prep or startegic thinking.

1

2

3

SECONDARY NEEDS

Tasks that are importnat but not primary.

ITEMS TO DISCUSS WITH A MENTOR

Challenges, Dark Side patterns or relations isolation.

THE ART OF SAYING "NO."

Which digital limits or non-essential requests will I decline to protect my family and soul?

Reflections and Joy

CULTIVATING JOY: 3 ITEMS FOR GRATITUDE

Gratitude guards the heart and restores perspective

1

2

3

GENERAL REFLECTION

Frre-form thoughts, shenanigans, and wound of ministry

INTEGRATION QUESTION

What small adjustment this week moved me toward mental and emotional health?

Soul Health

DATE(S)

SCRIPTURE MEMORY
Focus verse for this week

WORSHIP REFLECTION

How did I practice "often and solitary" time with the Father?

PRAYERS FOR YOUR PEOPLE

The flock entrusted to you.

PRAYERS FOR MY FAMILY

Spouse, children and grandchildren

PRAYERS FOR MYSELF

Personal burdens and requests

Rhythms and Renewal

BURNOUT DANGER LEVEL

Where am I on the road to burnout today?

DAILY RHYTHM CHECK

EXERCISE TODAY?
☐ YES ☐ NO

SPIRITUAL GIFTS PRIMARY?
☐ YES ☐ NO

HEALTHY EATING TODAY?
☐ YES ☐ NO

RESTORATIVE SLEEP?
☐ YES ☐ NO

SABBATH RHYTHM and RENEWAL

What "Protected Space" will I Safeguard this week?

PROCESSING CRITICISM

Discern truth, release falsehood, stay anchored in God's approval.

Formed for Ministry

PROCESS ITEMS CHECK

Rate how God is testing you this week (1-5 scale)

INTEGRITY CHECK
Character Consistency

(1)　(2)　(3)　(4)　(5)

OBEDIENCE CHECK
Willingness to follow God's lead

(1)　(2)　(3)　(4)　(5)

WORD CHECK
Applying Scripture to life.

(1)　(2)　(3)　(4)　(5)

EQUIPPING GOALS

Who am I training or coaching this week? (Moving from doing everything to equipping everyone)

RESPONSIVE MARGIN

How much "white space" have I left in my schedule to weep with those who weep?

Limits and Boundaries

PRIORITIES THIS WEEK (TOP 3)

Focus on predicable rhythmns like sermon prep or startegic thinking.

1

2

3

SECONDARY NEEDS

Tasks that are importnat but not primary.

ITEMS TO DISCUSS WITH A MENTOR

Challenges, Dark Side patterns or relations isolation.

THE ART OF SAYING "NO."

Which digital limits or non-essential requests will I decline to protect my family and soul?

Reflections and Joy

CULTIVATING JOY: 3 ITEMS FOR GRATITUDE

Gratitude guards the heart and restores perspective

1

2

3

GENERAL REFLECTION

Frre-form thoughts, shenanigans, and wound of ministry

INTEGRATION QUESTION

What small adjustment this week moved me toward mental and emotional health?

Soul Health

DATE(S)

SCRIPTURE MEMORY
Focus verse for this week

WORSHIP REFLECTION

How did I practice "often and solitary" time with the Father?

PRAYERS FOR YOUR PEOPLE

The flock entrusted to you.

PRAYERS FOR MY FAMILY

Spouse, children and grandchildren

PRAYERS FOR MYSELF

Personal burdens and requests

Rhythms and Renewal

BURNOUT DANGER LEVEL

Where am I on the road to burnout today?

DAILY RHYTHM CHECK

EXERCISE TODAY?
☐ YES ☐ NO

SPIRITUAL GIFTS PRIMARY?
☐ YES ☐ NO

HEALTHY EATING TODAY?
☐ YES ☐ NO

RESTORATIVE SLEEP?
☐ YES ☐ NO

SABBATH RHYTHM and RENEWAL

What "Protected Space" will I Safeguard this week?

PROCESSING CRITICISM

Discern truth, release falsehood, stay anchored in God's approval.

Formed for Ministry

PROCESS ITEMS CHECK

Rate how God is testing you this week (1-5 scale)

INTEGRITY CHECK
Character Consistency

(1) (2) (3) (4) (5)

OBEDIENCE CHECK
Willingness to follow God's lead

(1) (2) (3) (4) (5)

WORD CHECK
Applying Scripture to life.

(1) (2) (3) (4) (5)

EQUIPPING GOALS

Who am I training or coaching this week? (Moving from doing everything to equipping everyone)

RESPONSIVE MARGIN

How much "white space" have I left in my schedule to weep with those who weep?

Limits and Boundaries

PRIORITIES THIS WEEK (TOP 3)

Focus on predicable rhythmns like sermon prep or startegic thinking.

1

2

3

SECONDARY NEEDS

Tasks that are importnat but not primary.

ITEMS TO DISCUSS WITH A MENTOR

Challenges, Dark Side patterns or relations isolation.

THE ART OF SAYING "NO."

Which digital limits or non-essential requests will I decline to protect my family and soul?

Reflections and Joy

CULTIVATING JOY: 3 ITEMS FOR GRATITUDE

Gratitude guards the heart and restores perspective

1

2

3

GENERAL REFLECTION

Frre-form thoughts, shenanigans, and wound of ministry

INTEGRATION QUESTION

What small adjustment this week moved me toward mental and emotional health?

Soul Health

DATE(S)

SCRIPTURE MEMORY
Focus verse for this week

WORSHIP REFLECTION

How did I practice "often and solitary" time with the Father?

PRAYERS FOR YOUR PEOPLE

The flock entrusted to you.

PRAYERS FOR MY FAMILY

Spouse, children and grandchildren

PRAYERS FOR MYSELF

Personal burdens and requests

Rhythms and Renewal

BURNOUT DANGER LEVEL

Where am I on the road to burnout today?

DAILY RHYTHM CHECK

EXERCISE TODAY?
☐ YES ☐ NO

SPIRITUAL GIFTS PRIMARY?
☐ YES ☐ NO

HEALTHY EATING TODAY?
☐ YES ☐ NO

RESTORATIVE SLEEP?
☐ YES ☐ NO

SABBATH RHYTHM and RENEWAL

What "Protected Space" will I Safeguard this week?

PROCESSING CRITICISM

Discern truth, release falsehood, stay anchored in God's approval.

Formed for Ministry

PROCESS ITEMS CHECK

Rate how God is testing you this week (1-5 scale)

INTEGRITY CHECK
Character Consistency

(1)   (2)   (3)   (4)   (5)

OBEDIENCE CHECK
Willingness to follow God's lead

(1)   (2)   (3)   (4)   (5)

WORD CHECK
Applying Scripture to life.

(1)   (2)   (3)   (4)   (5)

EQUIPPING GOALS

Who am I training or coaching this week? (Moving from doing everything to equipping everyone)

RESPONSIVE MARGIN

How much "white space" have I left in my schedule to weep with those who weep?

Limits and Boundaries

PRIORITIES THIS WEEK (TOP 3)

Focus on predicable rhythmns like sermon prep or startegic thinking.

1

2

3

SECONDARY NEEDS

Tasks that are importnat but not primary.

ITEMS TO DISCUSS WITH A MENTOR

Challenges, Dark Side patterns or relations isolation.

THE ART OF SAYING "NO."

Which digital limits or non-essential requests will I decline to protect my family and soul?

Reflections and Joy

CULTIVATING JOY: 3 ITEMS FOR GRATITUDE

Gratitude guards the heart and restores perspective

1

2

3

GENERAL REFLECTION

Frre-form thoughts, shenanigans, and wound of ministry

INTEGRATION QUESTION

What small adjustment this week moved me toward mental and emotional health?

ABOUT THE AUTHOR

Phillip Andrade has spent more than forty years in ministry—long enough to have been a shepherd to teenagers, served as a missionary in Japan, and weathered two long-term senior pastorates in New England without losing his sanity or his sense of humor. Along the way, he earned a B.A. in Archaeology, an M.Div. in Theology, and a D.Min. in Leadership Development, proving that he is both somewhat educated and capable of sitting through very long monotone lectures.

To support his pastoral habit over the years, he has moonlighted as a police officer, graphic designer, and firearms instructor—which means he can preach a sermon, design the bulletin, and arrest you for not reading it thoroughly. He also dabbles in bladesmithing because nothing says "well-rounded pastor" like forging sharp objects.

He and his wife have been married for over forty years, have four children, and enjoy a plethora of grandchildren—a biblical word meaning "more than you can conveniently count." Now embracing the role of author, he brings together wisdom, shenanigans, and the wounds of ministry to encourage others to follow Jesus fully.

You can follow him, if you dare, at www.phillipandrade.com